Praise for *Awaken the Outl~~~*

"I'm a believer that too man[y]... cause they fear uncertainty. It's a ... book. He's onto something here." —**John Michael Morgan**, cons... ...author of the best-selling book *Brand Against the Machine*

"Want to live the life of your dreams? Know yourself. In a new and creative work, Ben Stroup reveals with insight the real search for significance through the mythic outlaw, magician, and hero residing in each of us. Since life's most formidable challenges lie not outside but inside each of us, discover here how to successfully release your inner hero and so live the life of your dreams. The path Ben Stroup provides is clear." —**Dr. Steve McSwain**, author, speaker, and contributor to Belief Net.com and *Huffington Post*

"Ben Stroup is a phenomenal writer. He combines biblical narratives and personal experiences in a way that makes the impossible seem possible. The spiritual journey is an adventure, and that's exactly what you'll find in this book." —**Pete Wilson**, senior pastor, Cross Point Church, author of *Plan B*

"Ben Stroup gives us names and new language to describe the compelling forces that drive us. Be ready to go on a deep inward exploration that leads to a reconciliation of the tensions. Experience the revelation of a divinely greater possibility and the gift to this world God intended you to be." —**Tami Heim**, president and CEO of Christian Leadership Alliance (CLA)

"Ben Stroup has a gift for creating powerful metaphors that disrupt our misconceptions and show us how to reach our potential.

This book will transform how you see yourself and everyone around you."
—**Ben Arment**, creator of STORY and author of *Dream Year*

"If we are made in God's image, we aren't relegated to live the life that others hand to us. Instead, each of us is uniquely designed to make a lasting imprint. Ben's book will disrupt your thinking and challenge you to discover and embrace your great adventure."
—**Tony Morgan**, author, blogger, and founder and chief strategic officer of The Unstuck Group

"Leaders are not afraid to go places that are unfamiliar to them. That's how they grow. This book proves our lives are a story waiting to be lived. Significance begins when we respond to the call to our own adventure and all that entails."
—**Wayne Elsey**, CEO, Funds2Orgs, and author of *Almost Isn't Good Enough*

"Risk and a different future begged me to come out and play. I did by becoming an entrepreneur . . . and I was welcomed into a journey that feeds my soul. Ben's book is an encouragement to those who have taken risks and to those who have yet to taste what risk can afford."
—**Bryan Miles**, CEO of eaHELP

"If, like me, you have ever found yourself restless and going through life simply checking the boxes as you were instructed to do from your earliest memories and yet you want more from life, then get this book now! Ben offers life-changing, faithful answers to perplexing challenges that will leave you inspired and motivated."
—**Rev. Dr. Dawson B. Taylor**, associate minister, Naples United Church of Christ

"Wow! Ben has done it again! Every time I've been with Ben or read anything he has written I have been encouraged to think dif-

ferently. This may be Ben's best work yet. Don't read this unless you want to be challenged. But, if you're ready for an adventure, start here."
—**Ron Edmondson**, pastor, church planter, and church leadership consultant

"This book isn't written for the reader looking to become a better version of themselves, rather, it's written for the individual who's prepared to transform into the person God created them to be. In this book, Ben makes the reader uncomfortable with where they currently are while also maintaining an excitement about where God is taking them."
—**Jordan Easley**, senior pastor, Englewood Baptist Church, and author of *Life Change*

"With a gifted mind and an enlightened spirit, Ben Stroup stimulates the reader to move from a restless identity to perceive the face of a true self. This 'gem' is an excellent read for personal growth and group discussion."
—**Dr. Geoffrey Butcher**, Episcopal priest and pastor

"We all have demands on our lives. It can feel like we go from boss to servant to dad to husband to son before breakfast! Ben's book releases us from the conventional thinking that's always been so limiting in our lives. He exposes what we've believed has held us back and offers refreshing options to move forward. If you're looking for fresh vision and tools to have success, you'll want to read this work."
—**Rob Ketterling**, lead pastor, River Valley Church, and author of *Change Before You Have To*

"Joseph Campbell for desk jockeys. Not ordinary desk jockeys, but the extraordinary ones, those who realize they're here for a reason, here to accomplish something great. This book will help the great ones find their greatness."
—**Jeff Brooks**, creative director at TrueSense Marketing, blogger,

and author of *The Fundraiser's Guide to Irresistible Communications* and *The Money-Raising Nonprofit Brand*

"With articulate and vulnerable self-reflection, Ben sets the course for those pondering the threshold of the 'narrow gate' into the uncharted territory of their own lives. This is a book I will recommend for anyone setting out to explore the depths of their own story and where that life is leading."
—**Dane Anthony**, spiritual director and former University chaplain, Belmont University, Nashville

"This must-read is large in its power to create personal breakthroughs. Ben Stroup combines mythology, biblical narratives, and personal experiences in a way that makes the impossible seem possible as you journey through your divinely designed life."
—**Dr. Kent Ingle**, president, Southeastern University, and author of *This Adventure Called Life*

"With an inspiring yet unusual approach, combining mythology, scripture, and personal story, Ben Stroup invites the reader to both find and live the true life implanted within them through divine design. If you are weary from status-quo living and find yourself hungry for significance, meaning, purpose, and breakthrough living, especially in seasons of transition, this book is a must-read for you. Be prepared to be awakened!"
—**Joel Mikell**, president, RSI Stewardship

"Life's complexity defies anyone to simplify it with a model or framework. Yet that is what Ben Stroup does with skill and grace in *Awaken the Outlaw*. This book will help you think with clarity so you can live with conviction. I commend it to you."
—**John Kramp**, senior vice president, HarperCollins Christian Publishing

Discover Your Process
for Transformation

★

Awaken
the Outlaw

Ben Stroup

Abingdon Press / Nashville

AWAKEN THE OUTLAW

DISCOVERING YOUR PROCESS FOR TRANSFORMATION

Copyright © 2015 by Benjamin W. Stroup

Library of Congress Cataloging-in-Publication Data

Stroup, Ben.
  Awaken the outlaw : discovering your process for transformation / Ben Stroup.
— First [edition].
    pages cm
  Includes bibliographical references.
  ISBN 978-1-4267-8957-1 (binding: soft back : alk. paper) 1. Self-actualization (Psychology)—Religious aspects—Christianity. 2. Typology (Psychology)—Religious aspects—Christianity. I. Title.
  BV4598.2.S85 2015
  248.4—dc23

                                                                2014043365

15 16 17 18 19 20 21 22 23 24—10 9 8 7 6 5 4 3 2 1

MANUFACTURED IN THE UNITED STATES OF AMERICA

To Brooke, Carter, and Caden
thanks for loving me through my uncertainty.
To the Restless Ones
never exchange your hopes and dreams
for the illusion of certainty today.

Contents

>   The reason we suffer so much from the chaos of life is that
> we hold to constructs that don't really exist. Instead, they are
> mere illusions of security and safety. The only true safe place is
> transformation. But it is less attractive because it is paved with
> destruction and death to ourselves and to all that we know to be
> true and complete.

>   The Outlaw refuses to accept the status quo. We wrongly as-
> sume that the authority in place is right, true, and just. It begins
> in kindergarten—or before then—when we learn to follow the
> leader. But what happens when we lose faith in the leader or the
> system altogether? It brings about a crisis of faith in which we
> must decide what to do next.

>   The Outlaw does not simply "follow the leader." We have
> been reluctant to challenge the authority and constructs that

govern our lives. If we just work hard, do the right things, then all the details will work out. So we assume a passive nature in life and wait to be told, invited, or promoted. Much of our lives are waiting to be lived. But by waiting we give away the rights that we posses through divine right.

The Outlaw sees people and authority for what they are—and what they are not. Most people deny the power that lies within them to create the life they want. The Outlaw recognizes contrast in life. He or she sees life in duality and recognizes that the normal flow of activities must be disrupted before change can take place. It begins with disrupting the world around you. Then you realize that the real disruption takes place when we look within.

The Outlaw is the embodiment of the restlessness we find within ourselves. We only move forward when we destroy that which is presently stable. The person who chooses the outlaw's journey is one who can never look back and—in turn—can never stay the same. The Outlaw is constantly moving, never settled, and is always looking for the next opportunity. It's scary and exhausting at the same time.

The Magician is known for his or her ability to bring about change and transformation. The only security we have is in the process of becoming new again each day as we are broken and made whole again and again.

The Magician sees beyond the physical world. Part of the transformation process is recognizing the constructs that we hold onto, thinking they are a safe bet and that they will never change. The truth is when something stops changing, it begins to die. We find the source of this in cellular biology, which tells us that to be alive is to be in a constant state of replication and renewal.

The Magician is not afraid of using divine forces to influence change in the physical world. Destroying the things that we hold onto tightly is frightening. It asks us to release all that we know to embrace that which does not yet exist. But every time we choose to destroy our security, we discover the illusions that were preventing us from moving forward in living into our divine potential.

The Magician reminds us that what is real can rarely be contained within the physical constructs of time and space. There is another dimension of reality. We chain ourselves to money, position, and power, when transformation reveals those things are passing and futile. As we begin to live life outside society's rules, we find freedom, adventure, and passion.

PART THREE | **THE HERO / 113**

The primary purpose of the Hero is to respond to the call of adventure, overcome temptation and trials, and return with enlightenment to better humanity. Faith is the gift we receive from the Hero; it is also the gift that we have to give others. The paradox of faith is that we don't understand faith until we give it away.

The Hero finds a belief system in his or her way of life. Every step of the Hero's Journey involves choices, decisions, and action. We only become who we were created to be when we act on what we know to be true. When we embrace the destruction that must take place and are open to transformation within, we can do the things we have been uniquely designed and gifted to accomplish.

Chapter Eleven | Rediscover the Creator Within / 142

The Hero participates in the creation process by bringing something back that benefits humanity. If we are created in the image of the Creator, then each of us also has the power to create. We are well aware of this as children but lose touch with our playfulness and imagination as we get older. The Hero recognizes that he or she has a specific role to play in bringing about change in the world.

Chapter Twelve | A Personal Offering / 157

The Hero acts on his or her behalf as well as on society's behalf. There isn't one Hero but many. We each have a journey to take. Our journey is our offering because it will lead us to become people who have the capacity to live into our divine potential and give ourselves to the benefit of others and—in turn—humanity. The greatest gift we have is ourselves.

Conclusion / 171

The problems with the world do not lie out there. Instead, they lie within. That which we hate most about the world is what must change within us before we can live into the full potential of our divine design.

Journal Exercise / 173

Acknowledgments / 177

Notes / 179

Suggested Reading / 181

About the Author / 183

Foreword

I cheer for certain kinds of folks.

I cheer for people who spend their days and hours devoted to their belief in things that we cannot see. My experience is that such people are the ones we can trust, the ones whose work can be counted on to be for the common good. They come in all manner of religious stripes, though the fact that they are religious is only part of it. It is something deeper, I think.

I cheer for people who are willing to make sharp observations and ask hard questions of themselves and others who seek to live a life devoted to the search for the Holy that is all around us. My journey has taught me that those are the people who will engage us in the conversation that leads to seeing the Holy more clearly, to letting go of the things that cloud our vision.

I cheer for people who are unafraid of wrestling with the truth of the gospel. My belief is that Scripture is a living and breathing thing, a word that demands that we grapple with it anew, generation after generation, even if it means some of us end up with a limp that reminds us of Jacob.

I cheer for people who do not flinch at telling their own truth, those willing to run the risk of being called out and proved wrong or clumsy or unskillful. My life has been made richer by those who have been so brave. The fact that I am still alive at all can be attributed to a handful of writers who had the courage to do just such a thing.

And I cheer for writers. Writing is not easy. It takes time and effort, courage and honesty, devotion and skill, talent and fortitude, hope and faith. There are people who live a life that provides an occasion for writing a book. Then there are those who dedicate their lives to only the making of books. I am one of them; it should surprise no one that I cheer for them.

So, I cheer for Ben Stroup. He is a pilgrim, a thinker, a truth teller, a writer.

I have been cheering for him for some years now, since the first long conversation we had walking up and down Church Street in a Nashville afternoon, going from bench to bench, telling stories and asking questions and becoming friends and wrestling with the Holy.

I recommend you read his work. I think you might come to cheer for him, too.

Robert Benson
At Sunnyside, in Kingdomtide, 2014

A Note to the Reader

Life is more than a prescribed set of behaviors and simple answers. Just listen to a child's questions about the world he or she is discovering and you'll be reminded how much more is going on than meets the eye.

I've always longed for clarity, purpose, and intention in my life. I've seen the cost of living a life that doesn't operate from our core. It's written on the empty faces of people I pass in the airport, the board room, and even church.

The search for purpose and meaning is, in my circles, often referred to as a search for God's will. Other contexts might refer to it as passion—the idea is that every human being has a purpose, a unique gift to offer the world, and a unique enlightenment that will ignite a similar journey in the people around us.

When I was told as a child I could be anything I wanted to be in life, I believed this to be true. But it's not—not because of situations and circumstances that are out of my control. Those surely can create obstacles. More important, I can't live up to that because my soul will not allow me to do just anything. That kind of life, a life I am forced to live out of my center, would be a very cold, dark place indeed.

Who am I? What is my gift to the world? How can I know what it means to be fully alive? These are ancient questions humankind has asked since the beginning of creation. But somewhere along the way I stopped listening for the answers buried in the stories I heard and started just giving answers, deciding somewhere along the way that we need "just the facts."

I've often recognized the wonder of a child in the life of an older, seasoned person. I've seen a season of answers morph back into a life thrilled again with questions and stories. In fact, I think it's possible that the older we get, the more comfortable we become with ambiguity, the same ambiguity that captures a child's imagination.

At times, I've craved clarity and certainty; in retrospect, it was uncertainty that created an atmosphere of stories that have guided me along my way. When the answers don't add up, all you have left is story.

I didn't realize that until I was sitting silent listening to a guru of sorts reading from the wisdom texts of the Bible—the same Bible I had heard read in my home, recited in church, and quoted in books. But what I heard sounded like it must have come from a different text altogether. I thought for a moment that maybe, just maybe, the guru mistakenly attributed his reading from another ancient text. But it was I who was surprised to learn that these were parts that must have been edited out from the Bible because they couldn't fit nicely inside three points and a poem. I'd heard very few sermons on these passages, yet I felt in that moment as if they were written for me. I couldn't get enough of them.

My hunger to understand life beyond the dimension of this natural world led me to two other significant voices: Joseph Campbell and Carl Jung. Together, their combined work about myth, archetypes, and the collective stories of my life and humanity as a whole provided something I desperately needed at just the right time. They taught me that I was not the first one to feel unsettled and as if I were wandering aimlessly in a desert.

The truth is, I needed more than answers to give me enough space to make sense of life while it hung in the balance between the question and the answer. And there is no better vehicle to soothe a wondering soul than stories.

In each of us lies something special. The challenge we must accept is the journey to uncover what that is for you and for me.

Seeing life and faith through the lens of myth and archetypes has provided a flexible way to interpret the world around me. The modern world is restless because many have lost any connection to the myths that guided humanity for centuries.

In our struggle to find a myth, we are running through substitutes that are distractions at best and destructive at worst. The tragedy is that unless we follow and respond to these mythic guides, we'll never become the hero who brings himself or herself as a gift back to society to improve the lives of everyone else.

As a little boy I remember praying that God would give me "eyes to see" and "ears to hear" the truth and the reality of my life, as the gospel text says, and to have the courage to follow the path given to me to take. Myth has become the gift, language, and vocabulary by which I have done this.

There are three figures within biblical text, cultural stories, and myths that stand out when grouped together: the Outlaw, the Magician, and the Hero. *The Outlaw* is the disruptor of all things normal. He or she appears when the powers of opposition are strong and someone must destroy something. *The Magician* is the figure who brings about transformation. There is a mystical and charismatic element to this person because he or she can bend impossible things within the scope of time and space to create another perspective or another opportunity altogether. Then we have *the Hero*. This is the person who has overcome temptation and returned to society to bring back knowledge and wisdom to benefit everyone else.

It was only when I discovered this combination as a late teenager and early twentysomething that I finally started to understand the different aspects, behaviors, and inclinations within me. Each of these mythic figures can conflict with each other unless they work together. No one was meant to live the life given to them by someone else. Instead, we are meant to live the life deeply implanted within us at the moment of creation.

If we are the image of God, then we are people who have the ability to destroy, transform, and create something new. When we are true to the Hero within us, the people around us benefit. But before we can become the Hero, we must destroy anything that might keep us from taking the journey and bringing about the transformation we have been given to make in the world.

The story of personal transformation exists both in mythology and sacred texts such as the Bible. Perhaps the most profound reality is just how much myth and Bible complement and color each other—so much so that I'll never read the Bible the same again. You will find both—myth and Bible—in my journey and in this book, in conversation with one another, in conversation with me, and, I hope, in conversation with yourself.

Introduction

We have all been told a lie. And we've accepted it at face value.

Who you are today is who you will
always be.
What you do is what you will always do.
And how you do it will stay relatively the
same.

We've believed this, bought into it, and accepted it as truth. But it was a lie.

I was in college during the Arthur Andersen and Enron debacles. There were two companies who embodied the American Dream: Work hard. Do your job. Don't do anything stupid, and we'll take care of you. Instead, their empires fell apart and left a load of innocent, shattered lives in their wake.

It wasn't too long after that when two planes rammed themselves into the sides of two iconic buildings in the middle of New York City. Everything changed that day. If there was any innocence left about our ability to live above the chaos happening around the world, it escaped within hours.

How could I continue to trust the expectations of others when it seemed that "sound wisdom" appeared to be neither sound nor wisdom? Everything seemed out of sync. Nothing seemed to fit just right anymore. It was like growing up—literally. Much like wearing clothes as a teenager. One day they fit. But the next time you try them on, the pants are too short or the shoes are no longer comfortable.

The idea that something didn't fit has been something that I lived with most of my life. As I've gotten older, it's become a restlessness driving me outside the scope and boundaries of many of the things I hoped would contain me. But people who step out of line aren't rewarded. To this day, power systems and institutions continue to try to intimidate those who might step out of line and move ahead along a different path.

But the irony in the midst of the story we find ourselves in is this: those who step out of line and survive—better yet, those who thrive—are then praised, trumpeted, and hailed as brilliant, extraordinary, and courageous. If this is true, why don't we all accept our own individual adventure to greatness?

Why? My opinion here: because we aren't really sure it's true. Yet our inability to pragmatically assure ourselves of this restlessness doesn't remove its nagging reality in our lives.

The world is not a better place because we develop the ability to follow someone else's rules. Instead, the world is a better place because we develop an awareness of the lies we tell ourselves and somehow take the risk of breaking through normal to find a new normal—one where our gifts, abilities, notions, and hunches lead us to a place of satisfaction and fulfillment.

The 1980s birthed a movement many label the me generation. There was a significant amount of upward momentum both economically and socially. People made more money. The professional ladder was in place and worked. And people were able to achieve a level of wealth their parents had only dreamed of. This transferred the confirmation we needed from within to the affirmation we found on the page of our own balance sheets. But, like any human construct, this wouldn't last either.

The Great Recession of 2008 created a new shockwave of activity. In a matter of days, balance sheets (the measure of success) were wiped away. Millionaires were homeless. The privileged felt poor. And an entire segment of the workforce had no idea what to do next.

This, for me, was like watching Enron fall and the Twin Towers be demolished, and any faith that remained in the institutions I was supposed to trust dissipated all over again. If the definition of our souls could be manipulated within a spreadsheet, then what motivation do we have to pursue the Hero's adventure we have all been called to complete? None. That is, until we have nothing left to keep us from the adventure we must take.

The Road Less Traveled is not just a book we have on our shelves. It is a real thing. In fact, it is the path everyone has walked who has ever changed the world in any measurable way.

And those who are willing to travel its path will feel everything that is human: pain, sadness, fear, and suffering. But those things only foreshadow what will come next: joy, excitement, courage, and enlightenment. We must accept both to be able to offer ourselves—not as experts but as people on a journey, pointing the way to those who come behind us.

The courage to leave behind our confidence, security, and protection leads to transformation and to the discovery that life—in abundance—has nothing to do with balance sheets, corner offices, or institutional structures. Those willing to live naked at the intersection of doubt and opportunity will discover that the pain of adventure is much shorter-lived than the desolation of indecision, or worse—the tastelessness of the one-size-fits-all approach to satisfaction and happiness.

Warning: this is an adventure that entails risk. It entails even destruction—setting aside cherished habits, sometimes even destroying idols. Should you decide to proceed, know that you won't remain the same. Proceed with reckless abandon. This is your great adventure.

PART ONE

The Outlaw

The greatest gift we can give ourselves is per-
mission to destroy that which we consider sacred.
Nothing truly sacred can be contained by anything
or anyone. Certainty—without divinity—is noth-
ing more than an illusion used in our human
attempt to contain that which is eternal.

CHAPTER ONE

The Way It Has Always Been

Judge a man by his questions rather than his answers.
—Pierre Marc Gaston de Lévis[1]

The greatest failure in life is not failure itself. It is, rather, our inability to approach the possibility of failure with reasonable excitement and embrace it as a path to success—however we choose to define that. I often choose to avoid failure and attempt success at all costs, wrongly assuming that failure is the opposite of success. But this couldn't be further from the truth. Failure is not the opposite of success but is deeply embedded in the experience of successes both big and small.

From as early as I can remember, I was socialized into following the leader. I learned to take cues from my parents, my brother, my teachers, my spiritual leaders, and my bosses. I didn't realize just how early boundaries were imposed on me until I was the one imposing the boundaries.

I am the father of two young boys. Dinner—or any meal for that matter—is similar to a chess match. You're not really sure what is about to happen, but you are paying as close attention to what you'd like to happen as what is actually happening.

Somewhere in the process of moving from a bottle to table food, we are taught to wait patiently, chew thoroughly, and try everything at least once. But those are the easy things. The hard things are sitting in your chair for the entire meal (or keeping all four chair legs on the floor), not showing everyone at the table the half-chewed food still in your mouth, or even not climbing across the table.

My oldest—as most first children do—adapted to the rules quickly. My youngest is another story.

Sitting down for a meal may be a time-honored tradition for some families. It's a game of trial and error in ours. My youngest believes it is an interruption in his otherwise busy schedule. He sits long enough to take one bite and then bounces out of the chair faster than a cat jumping out of water. He's always running somewhere. At dinnertime, that is typically around the table.

I'm confident both sons will leave an unmistakable mark on the world. But they will do so in very different ways. One will naturally write the rules, and the other will break them. Perhaps it is divine humor to provide such a cosmic counterbalance in our family.

As a husband and father, I want to provide a certain degree of order and stability. It is the expectation of society that parents—especially fathers, from my experience—provide that anchor or security. But you can't have any sense of security without establishing boundaries. There is very fine balance to strike between stability and confinement. This, I believe, is the truth we bump into at moments of interruption that seem to disrupt the natural order of things.

If you are willing to learn to live with a small amount of chaos in your life, you will open yourself up to moments of clarity that will ultimately lead to deep satisfaction in life. Whatever discomfort you experience is worth it.

The Order of Chaos

Authority and rule of law are important. We had to give up certain rights as individuals to come together and live in society with one another. This is the basic premise of the social contract that Locke, Hobbes, and Rousseau thought and wrote about. But somewhere along the way of learning to follow the leader down the hall to recess in kindergarten, we forgot to remind the little human beings in our care that boundaries are meant to protect us when the variables and circumstances are the known and predictable. But when the variables change or the situation is unknown, boundaries can contain us and hold us back from discovering new things about ourselves and the world around us.

Most of the rules we are taught are simple. Respect your elders, work hard, pay attention, follow the leader, and always do your best. The net result of these rules when we are young usually comes with some sort of instant gratification. We earn a cookie, extra time to play outside, or the chance to go pick out a new toy at the store. The benefits of following the rules remain fairly straightforward as we grow up. The distance between the act and the gratification isn't quite as instant, though, as we get older.

When we are in middle school, we are asked to decide if college is in our future. We need to know this because, at fourteen years of age, we must decide what college track we follow in high school. When we are eighteen, not even old enough to legally consume alcohol, we are asked to choose a degree program that will dictate our next four years of study and ensure our path to success postcollege. And, of course, we better not screw it up or we'll be in college forever and will send ourselves on a trajectory of failure that we will never be able to recover from.

It makes you feel all warm inside to check all those boxes, but life is not as cut and dry as the expectations imposed on us through community and cultural expectations seem to suggest. But it doesn't stop in college. The insanity continues.

With our degree in hand, we are asked to hand over the next three to four decades of our lives to a company that will offer us security, training, a steady paycheck, and opportunities for professional advancement. As long as we don't do anything criminal or unethical, the company will find something we can do reasonably well until retirement. During those three to four decades, we get married, buy homes and cars, raise children, send them off to college, and lean into and prepare for our retirement years when we have exhausted our use at said company.

That's a great life plan except for one thing: it's not true.

The truth is that some will never have the chance to go to college. And some who can are passing it by without blinking. For those who do go to college, our pursuit of the American Dream will most likely come with tens of thousands of dollars of debt. On career day, we are greeted not by the warm and loving arms of a company who wants to invest in us but a company who pays enough to get us to sign on the dotted line. And when we are no longer useful or it is possible to get the same amount of work in a cheaper or more efficient manner, our jobs will be eliminated.

Our golden retirement plans are left for us to fund. Pensions are something of a relic these days. And most family budgets will buckle under the cost of benefits alone. The house you buy will be mortgaged long enough to carry you into retirement or beyond. Family vacations are a luxury rather than an expectation.

Sometimes you feel like giving up. You feel depressed or angry because the world you thought you were promised isn't the world you seem to be living in. But when you set aside your despair, you realize there is a profound opportunity here. An opportunity to move beyond the illusion of certainty.

Life Is One Big Illusion

In every life there is moment when you realize some part of your life is an illusion. We carelessly demand the truth from others while letting ourselves off the hook from accepting the truth that is before us. This truth comes when all the variables of the equation are in place but the desired outcome doesn't match our expectations.

For me it came early in my pursuit of vocational ministry. I took my first church staff position in college at the ripe age of nineteen— just young enough to still believe innocently in the purity of peoples' intentions. While I was building bridges to students in the community who had never been part of church and to their families, others were frustrated with me. And to this day, I'm not sure I understand why.

It eventually led to verbal confrontation in a room full of angry and bitter people, which happened when the youth ministry was at its largest and most active. I thought I was about to be fired, and I had no idea why. But it became painfully clear that months of activity had been happening behind the scenes that culminated in this moment. All the while those who could have stepped in to help never said a word.

I wasn't old enough to know what was happening. While I had my eyes on the work I thought I was called to do, others had their eyes on me. This was not even an inquisition; it was a death squad intended to intimidate me and condemn me. And I didn't even understand why.

A few weeks prior to this meeting, I had learned of a list of names that was being circulated among a small group of restless and noisy church members who were not pleased with me. They couldn't argue with the amount of participation of the student ministry, so they focused their attention on me personally.

In the backdrop was my entire college experience, which was predicated on the plan to continue on to divinity school and spend my career in full-time ministry leadership. The presidential scholarship was awarded to me—in part—because of the declaration of this decision. My major was religion with an emphasis in psychology and ethics. My minor was biblical languages. By my senior year, I was assisting the professor with his first-year Greek class and reading Hebrew in public.

I did everything I knew to do to follow the rules, and that was supposed to be enough. But it wasn't; those rules failed me. And I suspect I am not the only one. Maybe your pursuit was something very different. Nonetheless, the details should sound strikingly similar.

In that church boardroom meeting, I realized this was not what I had signed up for. This wasn't the way it was supposed to be. I was doing God's work and reaching people who needed hope. Good things were happening, so why was this happening to me? But it wasn't the people I was helping who were eating me alive. It was the people who called themselves Christians and were dedicated church members.

It left me bitter and disillusioned. The next year was a long one with a long line of challenges that seemed unfair and calculated. I tried my best to keep my heart and faith intact, but I never was able to completely recover.

The confidence I had in my life's trajectory dissipated. All that I had prepared for seemed meaningless. Everything I was working toward seemed useless. I lost my balance—and my conviction—about the things I had hoped were true.

Whatever you want to call that entire experience, it sent me into a tailspin and into another direction I had neither asked for nor anticipated. All I knew was that I couldn't go back to "business as usual." That moment signaled a shift in my life that would, ultimately, shift everything.

The Truth of a Lie

I was scared, lonely, angry, and frustrated. All I knew to be true felt like a lie. What was I supposed to do now? The next steps that seemed so clear and calculated were now uncertain. I had never been more lost than I was during this time. Nothing seemed right. The pain of pressing on was too great. I would have to leave behind the dream I thought was mine for the taking. My only reasonable response was to leave behind the pursuit of professional ministry and exchange it for something else.

But what? I hadn't asked for this pivot; it had found me. And I knew I was not alone.

Abraham, that prominent patriarch and key figure of the Hebrew Bible, was challenged to leave behind the land of his fathers. Joseph—the prized son of Jacob—was sold into slavery by his brothers. Moses was compelled to leave Egypt. Paul was made blind on the road to Damascus.

Each of these remarkable characters embodies the fear and anxiety ancient people had with respect to the chaos of change. Growing up, I had heard their stories presented in a happy sort of way, as if they gladly and willingly accepted the pain and chaos of change. But now I realize it had to hurt them, confuse them, and frustrate them. Perhaps everything I was feeling at the time was also experienced by those individuals who also endured great disruption and transition and whose stories of faith were preserved for me and you.

If there had been Twitter, Facebook, and YouTube, we might have seen the evolution of these characters' situations more clearly. I wonder what Joseph would have tweeted from prison, or what Moses would have broadcasted from the mountaintop on YouTube, or even what Paul would have posted as a status update on Facebook as he went from church to church.

The changes these characters were asked to make were so significant that they marked a demarcation that rerouted the rest of their lives. Most people never experience this because they never allow themselves to think beyond the story they have been told or—more importantly—the stories they tell themselves.

When Life Breaks Down

The power behind "the way it has always been" is broken when we refuse to accept the variables and principles that make that story true. I wonder what Joseph thought when he was sold into slavery or what Moses felt when he had to leave the glory of Egypt and the position he held in the royal family. Paul was on the fast track to superstardom. Had there been a top-ten list of up and comings, he would have been on it.

All of these people painfully broke away from the story they had been telling themselves because unanticipated situations and circumstances forced them beyond their normal way of thinking.

The same is true for you and me. Few people seek to break the rule or destroy the illusions before them because they have yet to realize which stories are true and which ones are illusions. It isn't until a cataclysmic moment that we realize all we knew to be true has shifted—and its meaning along with it.

The irony is, the more we try to possess something, the more it will possess us. When we hold loosely to things of which we are certain, only then will we firmly gain that which will last forever.

The Outlaw Within

When those pivotal moments come, something is activated within us that we didn't know was there when we began. Call it gut or instinct. We know what we have to do even though seconds before the event the thought had never occurred to us.

There is a remnant within each of us that some call the Outlaw, that part of us that is activated and put into motion in times of great transition. The Outlaw is that part of every one of us who can no longer operate within the story we have been told. Whatever has happened has closed the door behind you. As much as you pound on it to open back up, you won't be able to retreat. The only option is to move forward.

Tapping into the Outlaw is the first step in the process of transformation. Until we are ready to destroy that which we know to be true, we are not ready to be transformed.

The Outlaw is a raw character who isn't accepted by the system but challenges it in every way. Much like the friction between a teenager and his or her parents, the Outlaw chooses to live in contention with the community. The Outlaw is feared by the rule followers because this person represents someone who willing to ignore the way it has always been. The Outlaw disrupts, challenges, and refuses to get entangled in the web of lies spread by the community because he or she sees them as they are—illusions based on "truths" that are not actually true. This understanding is the first step in the life of the the Outlaw.

There are consequences we must expect when we activate the Outlaw within us. We will be forced to confront ourselves and our participation in the creation of the story. True transformation can only take place within. Changing circumstances isn't enough; we must allow ourselves to be changed.

Another consequence is that you will be misunderstood. You will feel awkward, alone, broken, and likely angry. That's OK. Those are all the right feelings—even if they don't feel right. It's no different than a teenager separating from his or her parents. It's also not neat, clean, or tidy.

Finally, you will never be the same. That is part of the rush and excitement. You're not really sure what's next. You must learn to embrace chaos because it is the standard mode of operations now. That will never change. The story of stability must be rewritten to follow a new set of rules, and you'll discover those rules along the way.

Biology teaches us that cells must multiply and die. It is the process of life. Personal trainers teach that building muscle mass begins with tearing down the muscle that presently exists. Then when the muscle repairs itself, it is stronger than it was before. Life coaches teach us to stop doing the things that are holding us back from what we truly want to achieve.

The Outlaw may be a figure we want to avoid identifying with, but it is the mythic archetype we must live into if we are to journey through and beyond that which presently holds us back. At first, activating the Outlaw in your life will allow you to channel your hurt, frustration, and fear into something that will provide an outlet for your pain; but ultimately, it will cut a unique path for your transformation that will light up your soul.

The Courage To Let Go

When all that happened at church, during my college years, I was devastated. I knew I couldn't go on in my religious studies because my heart had been completely gutted. But I had absolutely no idea what I was going to do after graduation. My identity was wrapped around one path very tightly. I felt completely lost and as if I had let God down in a very substantial way.

I had to find another place to direct my passion, so I shifted my attention to a column I was writing for the university newspaper. It was the last time in my life I knew I could rage against the machine and not get fired or sued.

I had been asked to take the position after writing a guest column my junior year that the editor really liked. I received a ton of feedback from students, faculty, and even leaders in the community. It blew way past any expectation I had while writing it.

Writing that column became one of those most exciting things happening in my life during my senior year in college. As the weekly columns became more popular and widely read, informants began seeking me out with new information. That created a cycle of new information that kept growing my readership and taught me to discover I could write something that people wanted to create and inspired action.

The university administration tried to appease me. They placed me on a board that never met, they took me out to lunch so I would feel heard, and they even asked for my advice. It seemed as if they were following the textbook I was using in class to study social movement theory.

The Outlaw within me was fully activated, and, strangely, I had never felt more alive. I was asking big questions about myself and others. I was willing to take those questions into the realm of public opinion and allow them to be evaluated, dismissed, or acted upon. I was risking being completely ignored, but I was also risking the possibility of creating change. It was invigorating!

The Shape of Our Lives

Life has a way of shaping us whether or not we are prepared for it. It's coming. The best advice I've even been given to push through the pain is this: "Look it in the teeth, even if it bites back."

I was determined to see past the obvious and see things as they actually existed. That was true for what was happening not only on campus but also in my own life. I had many scary and dark days ahead of me for sure. But it was an adventure that was mine for the taking. I had been released from one story and given the opportunity to write a new one.

The Outlaw has a purpose. It just isn't consistent with the way it has always been. When the story is written from the point of view of the community, the Outlaw must be vilified. It is the only way to protect and preserve the community's permission system and the stories we tell ourselves.

But the perspective of the Outlaw and the stories he or she tells may be very different than we might first expect. We don't need a cape or a mask or even a weapon to be an Outlaw. There is one within each of us. And it is not a matter of *if* but *when* that part of us will be given the opportunity to appear.

The stories we have been given by our parents, pastors, teachers, and leaders must be exchanged for the stories God gives us to write. The function of the Outlaw is to make the transformation process possible by clearing out anything that stands in the way. In order to write our own stories, we need to risk boldly and fearlessly clearing out the false stories that have shaped us. This is brave, sometimes frightening self-work, but it is the necessary first step to a life of authenticity and freedom.

Chapter One in Review

To Reflect On

- The greatest failure in life is not failure itself. It is, rather, our inability to approach the possibility of failure with reasonable excitement and embrace it as a path to success.
- The stories we tell ourselves may make us feel warm inside in the moment, but they often leave us disappointed and wanting for more.
- In every life there is moment when you realize some part of your life is an illusion.
- The power behind "the way it has always been" is broken when we refuse to accept the variables and principles that make that story true.
- The irony is the more we try to posses something, the more it will possess us.
- When we hold loosely to things of which we are certain, we will firmly gain that which will last forever.
- There is a remnant within each of us that some call the Outlaw, which is activated and put into motion in times of great transition.
- Life has a way of shaping us whether or not we are prepared for it.
- The stories we have been given by our parents must be exchanged for the stories we will write ourselves.

- Letting go is the only path to transformation and the only hope we have of surviving in a world where chaos is normal, change is inevitable, and complacency is no longer an option.

To Ponder and Discuss

- List the rules you were taught and expected to follow from a very early age. Looking back on those rules, how have they influenced your life up to this point?
- Describe a time when you worked really hard, did all the right things, but things didn't work out. What happened? How did you respond?
- How would you describe the role of the Outlaw in your life?
- Thinking about a time when you decided to challenge conventional thinking, what inspired you to do it? What happened as a result?
- What is your life's story? Is it yours, or did you inherit or borrow it from someone else? If you had to rewrite your life's story, what would you change? Why?

CHAPTER TWO

Collective Complicity

You are a Christian only so long as you constantly pose
critical questions to the society you live in . . . so long as
you stay unsatisfied with the status quo and keep saying
that a new world is yet to come.

—Henri Nouwen

D reams have been part of my spiritual life for more than a decade now. I'm not sure what triggers them, but I can usually tell when a transition of some kind is coming by the frequency in which the dreams come.

I remember one dream where I was driving along in an official car of some kind. Perhaps it was a police car or a fire chief's car. The top was down, and I was in full dress uniform—the kind of uniform people only use for ceremonial occasions. Someone was riding in the front bench seat with me. I'm not sure who, but I was aware of his presence.

I came to an official roadblock. The officer approached my vehicle, immediately recognized me, and spoke with great respect. He seemed nervous, as if I were someone of particular importance and rank. I remember feeling strange about the whole thing because I didn't know the officer, nor did I know how I ended up in this uniform and car. I was even uncertain about where I was headed. But it was the uniform that became my ticket to bypass the roadblock ahead. I was signaled to move on ahead.

The power of dreams is not what they tell you about other people but what they reveal about yourself. One might consider it an honor or perhaps a foretelling of some great achievement I might experience in the future. I understood it to mean something entirely different. I was wearing a uniform I didn't ask for, driving in a car that marked me in a particular way in which I was not comfortable, and had authority that I didn't believe was rightfully mine.

I believe everyone wears a uniform. Some wear uniforms that are given to us by others and some wear a uniform that we have given ourselves. A uniform represents an identity and rank. A formal, or dress, uniform displays our greatest achievements in moments of particular importance.

Perhaps the questions we all eventually ask ourselves are: what uniform are we wearing? And what does that uniform tell us about who we believe we are and how other people see us?

The Outlaw wears a very different uniform from the community that has given him or her that name. It is a uniform not recognized by the masses. When something (or someone) doesn't fit in line with the expectations of the majority, the idea or person is deemed a threat. That can be a very scary and unnerving experience, even for an Outlaw.

But the greatest threat to transformation is our inability to be comfortable living on the outside of other people's expectations. The spiritual life is one that exists in constant tension between the inner and outer world. It is not a comparison between you and someone you know, admire, or even despise, as much as it is a direct conflict between the expectations we inherit from others and the person we were created to be from the beginning.

The Divine Breath

The story of creation as told in the first chapter of Genesis is a beautiful picture of the divine fingerprint we contain from the very beginning, the moment of our great innocence and vulnerability. The Creator bends over and breathes life into humankind. The Creator breathed life into me and you. In doing so, we were left with a remnant of the Creator within us. Our task is to get past the layers of external expectations and assumptions that cover our true selves and discover who we have been created to be.

There is no way around it. Destruction, separation, and abandonment are the things that must come first in order for us to be prepared to enter the transformation phase. A runner doesn't begin training for a marathon by running long distances. On the contrary, a runner begins by establishing a baseline of running activity, speed, and endurance that, in turn, prepares the runner to begin the intense training a marathon demands.

Perhaps the greatest threat to discovering our true selves is not others or even our own circumstances, however impossible they may seem. Indeed, it would be a tragedy to willingly put on a uniform you were never meant to wear to gain access to a life you never really wanted to live. When we allow this to take place, we participate in what I call collective complicity.

Sometimes it is easier to just move along with the majority. There is great resistance when we don't. We tell ourselves as children, "Sticks and stones may break my bones, but words will never hurt me." No matter how much we try to convince ourselves of that, there is a need deep within everyone to be accepted, affirmed, and approved.

We begin our lives trying to earn the approval of our parents, siblings, and family. Then we go to preschool and discover we want to be approved and accepted by our friends and teachers. As we get older and discover the power of human connection, we are naturally attracted to other people. We strive for their approval, too.

When we go to college, we want approval and acceptance by friends, teachers, and staff. If we play sports, perform on a stage, or even volunteer at a nonprofit, we want to earn the approval from the people we encounter along the way. It doesn't stop there. We want the approval of our bosses, children, faith leaders, and spouses. And the worst is our incessant obsession with approval from people we don't even know.

We buy bigger houses, nicer cars, take more extravagant vacations simply because we need to outdo and—by default—earn the momentary admiration of the neighbors. It is a futile race most of us chose to participate in. Whatever level to which you are involved, you are part of the collective complicity that is keeping you from preparing the way for you to discover who it is that you were given to be the moment the breath of life filled your body at birth.

The Power of Permission

I don't even remember when I started saying this, but I do remember it being an intentional decision. Shortly after my oldest son was born, I started to whisper in his ear: "I love you, and I'm proud of you. I will always love you, and I will always be proud of you." I still do that as often as I can to this day and continue the effort with our youngest child.

I want my children to know there are no boundaries on my love and admiration for them. Even when they could do nothing for themselves, I was proud of them and loved them. And when they can one day do everything for themselves, I will be proud of them and love them. I want those words to give them permission to explore life and hopefully discover themselves in the process. It is, I believe, the greatest gift that I could give them. My deepest desire is that they would not become so entangled in the expectations of others that they must spend decades scraping off the junk that is keeping them from their own journey to transformation.

It's easy to look at the Outlaw with condemnation. The truth is the Outlaw exists within each of us. It is the part of us that we aren't sure what to do with. It is the curiosity we are fearful might lead us in a direction that is unknown. It is the fire that burns within us that we try not to let consume us. It is the adventure we try to not give into because we aren't sure what would happen next.

So we exchange our God-created selves for the uniforms we have been given that tell us where we will live, who we will love, how we will worship, and what vocation we will pursue. It is easier to forgo the Outlaw experience. The only problem is that we can't get to transformation without first destroying the things that hold us back from beginning the process.

I have spent most of the last decade regretting the decision not to continue into professional ministry. What I have realized is that the source of my regret is not passing on a vocational opportunity but the comfort I would experience by accepting a role that is so clearly defined. That was a uniform I wanted to wear so badly that everything along the journey that prevented me from doing so was an interruption and an unnecessary obstacle.

My painful experience in local church ministry in college forced me to let go of a uniform I had clung to for dear life. And it sent me wandering into a wilderness that exposed just how little I knew about myself and my place in the world.

I completely understand why people forgo the experience of being the Outlaw—why we sometimes cling to that familiar uniform instead of setting it aside. It is dark, lonely, and not very pleasant.

I sometimes take comfort in the knowledge that the children of Israel wanted to go back to Egypt, that the spies with Joshua were overwhelmed by the giants in the land, and that even Jesus prayed that he would not have to die. If those appointed by God—and God in the skin of Jesus—had momentary desires to pass on "the cup" that had been given to them, then why would any of us expect our lives to be any different?

It is not an uncommon theme in ancient stories, including biblical literature, to see that suffering must come before resolution.

Burying a Nun

During a particularly dark season, I had another dream.

I was with two other guys. We were digging a grave for someone. I had a shovel in my hand and was almost ready to place the body in the ground. I was unsure if I was in a cemetery or why I was the one doing the digging and feeling responsible for this person.

When it was time to put the body in the ground, I picked it up, draped it over my shoulder, and placed it in the grave. When I stood back up, I realized it was the body of a nun. She was in her traditional dress. She appeared dead. I paused for a moment. I'm not sure why. I wasn't a priest, so I didn't have anything in particular to say.

I picked up the shovel and started to cover up the body when I saw her eyes open. It felt as if she were looking directly at me and saying, "Stop this. I'm not dead."

The meaning of this dream to me was profoundly insightful. I tried to bury an official representative of a faith and God that I wasn't sure still existed. That faith and God were a deep part of who I was, and that part of my identity felt void. So burying the nun made sense. What is even more startling is that this nun, who appeared dead, opened her eyes and spoke to me.

If we cannot handle paradox, then we have no business in pursuit of transformation. What seems dead is alive. And what seems alive can appear dead. My faith and belief system in the Source of Life were still intact. My faith and belief in a particular expression of my divinely given breath were limited to one construct—vocational ministry. I was happy to complicitly live into that role because it was familiar. But as good as that plan would have been, I had concocted it based on a very limited view and scope of possibility.

In short, I was tied to a uniform more than I was tied to a pursuit of significance, meaning, and my true self.

The Bible often talks about the path to God being the straight and narrow. I might have written that differently. Yet, the Bible repeats stories of the path to God as full of unexpected twists and turns, unforeseen roadblocks, and impossible crossings. The reason so few ever trudge down this path is the fear of what they might discover about themselves along the way.

Transformation is not nearly as romantic of an idea as we like to think it to be. We like to think of it as a caterpillar that becomes a butterfly. That's nice, but it's not consistent with transformation in any form I've observed or experienced.

Transformation is messy, chaotic, full of surprises, and layered with setbacks. Within those messes, changing habits, behaviors, and perceptions is one of the most holistic and impossible things you can ever attempt. It will not feel right, normal, or comfortable for a long time. But as the "fake it until you make it" philosophy behind addiction programs teach, you have to continue to move forward by moving though.

The physical separation the Outlaw has with the community provides a great metaphor for how we can understand this phase of transformation. The Outlaw within us must separate the complicit life from our fully alive state. It can seem like an out-of-body experience at times. And it will be hard to tell one from the other. We must become uncomfortable with ourselves before we can begin the process of being changed.

I can think of no greater obstacle than to challenge the norms of our family traditions, our faith traditions, and our cultural expectations. Those are difficult because contained within them are layers of junk that must be cleared before we can hope to begin seeing clearly. But the promise we have is if we take the journey, we will not be disappointed. Jesus promised us the abundant life. Open your hands. Open your heart. Take off your uniform and the subsequent expectations that have been imposed on you—or that you have imposed on yourself. It's only then that you can begin the self-work necessary to fully activate your soul. The paradox is that the only one holding you back from living into that fullness is you.

Chapter Two in Review

To Reflect On

- The power of dreams is not what they tell you about other people but what they reveal about yourself.
- Everyone wears a uniform. Some wear uniforms that are given to us by others, and some wear a uniform we have given ourselves.
- When something (or someone) doesn't fit in line with the expectations of the majority, the idea or person is deemed a threat.
- The greatest threat to transformation is our inability to be comfortable living on the outside of other people's expectations.
- Destruction, separation, and abandonment are the things that must come first in order for us to be prepared to enter the transformation phase.
- To willingly put on a uniform you were never meant to wear to gain access to a life you never really wanted to live is a tragedy.
- Too often we would rather be complicit with the expectations of others than pursue the path that was breathed into us at the moment our lives began.
- The only one holding you back from living into the fullness of who you are is you.

To Ponder and Discuss

- What uniform are you wearing? What does it say about you?
- If you had to pick a uniform to wear every day, what would it be? Why?
- In what ways are you complicit with the expectations of others? In what ways do you challenge the expectations of others?
- Describe an experience where you felt like you were on the outside. What happened? How did you feel? What did you do in response to that experience?
- What role does paradox play in faith?

CHAPTER THREE

Denial Is Not a Life Strategy

Looking means a contemplative willingness to see what is there in front of us without prematurely interpreting what we see.

—Alan Jones

It's sad to watch people who have given their souls away in exchange for stability and security realize they traded their lives for an illusion. Just ask the professional worker who was a few years from reaching full retirement when her company let her go. Just ask the husband and wife who are now empty nesters and just realized their relationship is as empty as their home is now. Just ask the college graduate who took out loans to attend college with a promise of a better future and a good paying job who has been unable to find meaningful work for three years—or longer.

We keep telling ourselves the same story—follow the rules, do the right things, avoid bad decisions—but the outcomes of our choices don't seem to be getting better. At best, the future seems bleak. And far too many people are hoping life will go back to the way it was. When things were simpler, everyone seemed happier, and so much more about life was predictable.

Risk, chaos, and obstacles have always been part of the journey through life on earth. We've just worked so hard to insulate ourselves from it that returning to a state of awareness about those characteristics feels a bit like peeling a scab off a wound that has yet to fully heal. So we hunker down, wait, and hope for the best.

Dante wrote about coming to a dark woods in midlife. That dark woods, I like to think, was his realization that things had shifted— that the reality of his life was different than what he had anticipated. What do we do when we notice that things have shifted? Pivot along with the shift—sometimes gracefully, sometimes awkwardly. But the pivot is how we find true north, and how, ultimately, we find our balance again.

The Promise of the Professional Life

I remember my first job out of college. It was with one of those $600 million annual revenue companies that touted security and stability. I was told that if I just worked hard, followed the rules, and waited my turn, then I would advance through the ranks and could retire in comfort. That may have sounded good to the corporate employee leading new employee orientation, but for a twenty-two-year-old facing—at least—another forty-five years of work, that seemed like a death sentence.

I spent the first twenty-four months of my professional life with my foot on the clutch and the gas pedal—at the same time. If you've ever done that before, you know that all you accomplish is excessive revving of the engine, eventually producing smoke, and burning up precious gasoline. In short, you make a lot of noise, risk a lot of damage, and accomplish absolutely nothing. That's exactly how I felt. My job was to wait until someone else died or retired for me to get my "big break." I wasn't buying it.

As I started to share my frustration with others who were a little ahead of me, they smiled, patted me on the head, and told me to wait my turn. I don't wait well. I am the guy who would rather pay for overnight shipping then wait a week and save twenty bucks because when I want something or need something, I want it now. I even had one manager tell me that I needed to have about ten years of work experience before I could be considered for the management program. What?! That was a lifetime.

Keep in mind that just a few years earlier, Enron and Arthur Andersen had their debacles. People who had invested decades in companies that were supposedly infallible and bullet-proof suddenly had little to nothing to show for it. I never gave myself the opportunity to believe that any company would take care of me.

While in college, a mentor gave me a little book by Tom Peters, a well-known management consultant. It was titled *Brand You!* In it, Tom captured a mantra that summed up how I still feel about life today. He writes colorfully (and I've adapted here): "Do cool stuff! Every flippin' day! Or die trying!"[1]

That book changed my life. Tom talked about the importance of seeing every opportunity as temporary. He explained that professionals should measure life by projects that have remarkable characteristics about them.

Even if we are an employee on someone else's payroll, we are exchanging our time and talents for the opportunity to improve our personal asset portfolio. And Tom wasn't just talking about money. He was talking about skills, experience, perspective, and so on. This way of thinking made sense to me.

The Difficult Path of Growth

I remember a time when I was facing a decision in college that was of particular importance at the time. I asked a sage professor what he would do. His response was consistent with the guru figure he had become for so many of us on campus. He said, "When you face a choice between two things, pick the one that is the most difficult and scares you the most. It is the one that will provide you the most opportunity for growth."

With his advice in hand, I decided I would commit to something long enough to learn as much as I could, achieve as much as I could, and perform as well as I could. Then, when I had nothing left to learn, no more opportunities to grow, and no more projects to build on, I would fire myself and move onto the next task. I wanted nothing more than to find ways to constantly be challenged, intrigued, and engaged in my professional life. And my current position just wasn't cutting it.

The trouble was I didn't have people around me who applauded my restlessness. They told me to sit down, shut up, and wait my turn. But I refused to accept that as a mode of operations for my life. I knew it would cost me, but I was much more confident in my ability to create stability and security for myself than I was in any organization.

I reached out to a local newspaper about becoming a newswriter but was told that without a journalism degree, I had no hope of being considered. And I even reached back out to a few divinity schools. All of them reserved their full scholarships for full-time students. Even though I could show them how I could finish the degree within the allotted time, I didn't fit the mold they wanted. (This is a recurring theme for me, by the way. Most of the time no one knows what to do with me.)

So I did what anyone with a religion degree who was also fluent in biblical Greek and Hebrew would do: I found a job selling payroll software to midsized businesses. After living in the landscape of traditional publishing in the early 2000s, I knew it was a business that simply wasn't moving fast enough for me. I was already stoking a freelance business on the side that I had started in college. I wanted to be on my own as a freelance writer, but there was no table at career day that advertised such a position. My best guess was that if I could learn how to sell, then I could do anything. Everyone is a salesperson, even if that is not your formal title or position.

I was young and full of myself. This move seemed completely out of sync from the outside looking in. But in that moment, it made perfect sense to me. And I felt lucky. I wasn't forced out, fired, or sent packing by my employer. I left on good terms and with the door of opportunity wide open in the event that I fell flat on my face.

That move was the absolute best one I could have made. It taught me more about myself than I ever could have imagined. And it gave me the courage to keep pressing forward. It opened up new doors for me as I continued to search and seek for my place in the world.

Escaping God

My story may sound as if all of this was easy. It wasn't. And to add a degree of complexity to the matter, I was married. My wife was—by default—on this journey with me.

I had very little to do with the God of my youth during this time. I wanted to get as far away from my faith as I could. Nothing seemed right on the inside. If my life appeared chaotic on the outside, my inward self was in even deeper turmoil. My entire identity had been wrapped up in one particular career path, and it seemed no longer available to me.

It showed up in every way: my posture, my interests, my temper, and my general attitude about life. I had committed at a very young age to spending my life doing the responsible thing at the expense of doing the thing that really ignited my soul. But what was I supposed to do now? The door was locked. I no longer fit in a place that seemed so comfortable. And no one seemed to understand just how traumatic this was.

One Saturday morning I was at the car shop getting my oil changed. From where I was sitting, I could see into the area where the mechanics were working. It seemed like an endless stream of bays where cars were elevated on hydraulic lifts. They seemed to be working fast and furiously. Each one of the mechanics wore a uniform with his name on it. I remembering thinking about how much easier life would be if I could just find the right uniform with my name on it. Then I would know what to do, when to do it, and how to do it. I wanted to stop this incessant tape in my head from spinning.

I didn't have a language for it at the time, but I was disassociating myself from what was familiar around me. I was living into what it meant to experience being an outsider, an Outlaw. My appearance didn't change. I didn't put on a physical mask and change the color of my clothes to black. But I did intellectually, spiritually, and mentally disconnect in an attempt to save myself from further pain. When I looked up, I realized I was drifting further and further away from what I had known was comfortable and familiar.

I wanted to be anybody but me. I had done all the right things, followed all the rules, and yet I felt stuck. And worse, I didn't feel like I could be the person my wife needed me to be. I was so messed up inside that I couldn't be her anchor. And it was unfair for me to expect her to be mine.

Alternate Reality

When we begin to take off the uniform we have been given, we begin to see life differently. There is an element within us that is awakened to another perspective. Somehow we begin to adopt another point of view.

Don't expect people to understand what you are going through. My experience tells me there is only a small percentage of people who are brave enough, courageous enough, and daring enough to take this journey. You could call it a loss of innocence. And you can choose to embrace it on your own terms or wait until life slaps you in the face and you are forced to come to terms with it.

Of course, you always have the option to deny the Outlaw within you. You can drown it with excessive eating and drinking, working, exercising, or any number of things. Your tool of destruction is yours to decide. But as Lt. Col. Frank Slade (played by Al Pacino) says in his epic soliloquy in *Scent of a Woman* (1992), "There is *nothin'* like the sight of an amputated spirit. There is no prosthetic for that."[2]

Denial Is the Easy Way Out

Denial is a sure way to skip out on the life that was breathed into you at the moment of your creation. Within you rests the ability to create—and live—the life God has gifted you with. But you must decide whether or not it is a journey you are willing to take. The initial phase is perhaps the most bloody of them all. It's the part where you must break open the wound before it will heal properly. It's the part where you must willingly accept the pain of change. And it's the moment you must acknowledge that failure is always an option.

One night I dreamed I was driving around what I thought was a shopping mall. When I started driving, there was a lot of light. People were everywhere. And it seemed like everyone had decided to come to the mall that day. Traffic was terrible. People were rude. And there were the trolls driving up and down the aisles looking for the perfect parking spot.

I continued to drive around the mall. I really had no idea where I was going. As I continued driving, I realized it was getting darker and darker outside. There were fewer and fewer people. And I had no idea how to get back to where I had started. My heart began to race. My palms became sweaty. I realized in that moment I was lost, scared, and in trouble.

I could not have dreamed a more vivid representation of the fear that keeps people from living into the life they were destined to lead. Denial is the most readily used escape mechanism for the pain of transformation. If you can deny it long enough, perhaps you will stop hearing that voice within you, stop feeling that longing and restlessness for something more, and stop believing change is possible. But the flip side of that is that you will have stopped living, too. Some other obsession will occupy your energy, but it won't be the life force you so deeply desire.

Denial is a powerful tool the human mind possesses. It can alter reality, make us accept things that are not true, and keep us from reaching for our potential. It is a coping mechanism that also has the ability to completely erase our sense of self.

Natural Disruption

The opposite of denial is not truth; it is disruption. And anyone who disrupts the normal flow of activities, life, and expectations is deemed a deviant, a troublemaker, and a problem creator. If life is a system, then we are just supposed to know our roles, live into them, and do our part to keep the wheels of life spinning. At least this is what we are told by those with authority over us.

When we refuse to deny the longing within us, we also accept the reality that disruption will come. It is how the Outlaw interacts with the community he or she has separated from. The Outlaw can't help from stumbling over permission systems that fit the cadence of the stories that keep everyone in line and consistent with the way it has always been.

Some have called me a natural disruptor. No matter what I seem to do, I always find away to trip over someone else's rules. I don't even have to work at it. It just happens.

Shortly after starting my first professional job, someone described the company's open-access policy to upper management. We were encouraged to find the contact information for people we'd like to meet and reach out to them. This person commented that some have even been brave enough to get appointments with the president of the company. This was a four-thousand-employee company, so it wasn't like the president's office was just down the hall.

I took him at his word. If I wanted to be successful, then I had to surround myself with successful people, right? I reached out to most of the vice presidents, thinking that would be a good place to start. I met with them during my lunch break, so it wasn't a very long meeting.

All was going well when somehow my direct manager found out about it. He told me that I shouldn't be bothering them and should bring any issues or concerns directly to him. I explained that it had nothing to do with him or my current position. In fact, it didn't have to do with me at all. I simply wanted to interview successful people to uncover the secret sauce to their success. He didn't buy it.

And then there was the time when I was doing research to launch a new product line. I started to meet with people throughout the company and ask them questions to help me flesh out the data I was collecting and my assumptions about the project. I would meet with one person, get the information or perspective I was looking for, and then ask for one referral. It really was a lot of fun because I was able to meet a lot of different people.

One referral came to me that I was very excited about. We met, and I walked away feeling like it was a very positive meeting. It was but a few days when my department director called me into his office. Apparently, I had asked the right question to the wrong person. That individual thought I was attempting to launch something that would negatively impact his area. (He gave me too much credit for my intelligence-gathering acumen.) That individual sent an SOS signal to his vice president, who then contacted the vice president of my division, whose message eventually trickled down to me. (Forget picking up the phone and addressing me directly.)

Denial Delays Progress

Disruptors are accepted in certain contexts. You want law enforcement to disrupt the plot of criminals and those who seek to do harm. You want doctors to disrupt the negative affects of a disease or illness. You want psychologists to disrupt the negative thoughts in our minds that inhibit progress. But in most contexts, disruptors are considered troublemakers and are made out to be outlaws, lone rangers, and those who are only in things for themselves.

Normal is no longer normal. The quicker you can begin live into the tension between what is passing away and what is being created, the sooner you'll be able to notice the nuances that provide contrast to this life. And contrast is what is necessary to separate yourself from old patterns and habits and begin to form new ones.

You can't expect to repair a car without taking it apart. You can't expect to change the batteries in a toy without unscrewing the battery plate. And you can't expect to change yourself without dismantling what you believe is intact.

The most troubling part of our lives that we must let go of is the illusion of security and stability in the things we have been told are supposed to make us feel secure and stable.

I am learning that true stability and security are found in beginning to tell a different story where transformation and change are understood as the very process you can count on to move forward.

Chapter Three in Review

To Reflect On

- We keep telling ourselves the same story—follow the rules, do the right things, avoid bad decisions—but the outcomes of our choices don't seem to be getting better.
- Risk, chaos, and obstacles have always been part of the journey through life on earth.
- Life as we know it has shifted.
- When we begin to take off the uniform we have been given, we begin to see life differently.
- Don't expect people to understand what you are going through.
- You can choose to embrace life on your own terms or wait until it slaps you in the face and you are forced to come to terms with it.
- Denial is a sure way to skip out on the life that was breathed into you at the moment of your creation.
- Within you rests the ability to create—and live—the life you want.
- Denial can alter reality, make us accept things that are not true, and keep us from reaching for our potential.
- The opposite of denial is not truth; it is disruption.
- When we refuse to deny the longing with us, we also accept the reality that disruption will come.

- The quicker you can begin live into the tension between what is passing away and what is being created, the sooner you'll be able notice the nuances that provide contrast to this life.
- The only stability and security in this new normal is learning to tell a different story where transformation and change are understood as the very process you can count on to move forward.

To Ponder and Discuss

- Identify two of your biggest disappointments in the last twelve months. What happened? Why did it matter? What did you learn about yourself?
- How does denial hold us back from transformation?
- When is disruption a good thing? When it is not? How do we know the difference?
- If you could change one thing about your life right now, what would it be? What is holding you back from making that change?
- If change is constant, how does our life story need to adapt?

CHAPTER FOUR

The Evolution of
Ourselves

There is no such thing as immaculate perception.
—Stephen M. Kosslyn and Amy L. Sussman

If Merriam-Webster needed a face to supplement its definition of *restless*, it would be mine. On our tenth wedding anniversary, Brooke and I realized we had purchased eight vehicles since we were married. I carry two phones with me because I like tinkering with technology. I regularly change the setting on a variety of gadgets, take different routes to get to familiar places, and adjust my playlists on a whim.

But it doesn't stop there. In the first ten years of my professional life, I held five different positions within two separate companies. That's not counting the freelance business I was stoking on the side.

Change is a normal mode of operations for me. That doesn't mean I can't focus, nor does it mean that I don't have the ability to perform and get results. What that means is I'm on a constant search for what's next. The temptation I have to fight against is not getting pushed out the door but missing out on the next great opportunity because I let it slip by unnoticed. There is always a sense of adventure—or stress and anxiety—that seems to color my outlook on life.

My wife, on the other hand, is not as open to change as I am. I'm pretty sure I stress her out most of the time. And when I tell her I've started dreaming a lot, she has learned to hunker down and hold on. She knows that change always follows a series of dreams.

Unlike me, she is the picture of stability. She is risk averse, a deeply systematic saver, and singularly focused on what she wants to accomplish and who she wants to be. I envy her sometimes. Life, for her, seems so clear and settled. Perhaps it is some divine humor that God demonstrated in bringing us together. The very things that have created the most tension in our relationship are also the things we love about each other.

A Book Full of Misfits

The biblical characters I seem to connect with most are misfits. They make up their own rules and seem to operate outside the acceptable expectations of others. It is a good thing the Bible is filled with them. It makes me feel at home. (Isn't it strange how culturally we connect being a follower of Christ with following the rules, when that wasn't a characteristic of most of the "heroes" from our sacred texts?)

Truthfully, Jesus was a misfit. People who follow the rules don't draw crowds, challenge established protocols, claim divine authority, confront corrupt governments and leaders, and end up getting themselves killed. It's easy to read the ancient texts and scoff at the people who rejected him, but many would do the same today. I bet if Jesus were alive today, he would not be someone most Christians would want to follow.

Of all the characters I have come to admire and appreciate, Jonah is at the top of the list. He was God's prophet to God's people. Jonah was respected and admired. As God's voice, he was supposed to call people back to a lifestyle of faithfulness and spiritual practice. And he obviously was very effective at it.

So one day God asked Jonah to go to a particular place and tell the people there to stop living destructive lifestyles and start following his God. There was only one problem: Jonah didn't like the people there, so he decided to opt out of God's design. Jonah, being the faithful servant of God that he was, decided to travel in the completely opposite direction.

It turns out his travel plans didn't work out quite as planned, and the joke was on him. Jonah found himself in the belly of a whale. Well, we really don't know what kind of fish it was, but it obviously was a big one. And he was there for three days before he decided to change directions and proceed with God's original travel itinerary.

Every time I eat fish, I wonder if Jonah smelt what I do. I take great comfort knowing that even God's appointed voice on earth can attempt to negotiate the grand design of life. I think Jonah and I would make great friends.

Escaping God

Jonah's story is a perfect metaphor for the Outlaw. The harder we try to run away from something, the more likely that we'll run right into it. And when we do, we'll feel trapped, held back, and frustrated. But somewhere in the pushing and the pulling, in the feeling of being stuck with no progress, we'll emerge with a new perspective.

Water is a beautiful metaphor for the source of our strength. It is much stronger and more stable than we might first think. And the story of living in the belly of a whale gives us an indication that we must first digest and process who we are becoming before we are ready to go there.

Jonah had to go deep into the waters where there is stillness, darkness, and solitude in order to become transformed. If that doesn't depict the experience of the Outlaw, I don't know what does. I find this idea intriguing but not unusual. We see it played out in the lives of some very familiar biblical characters.

Jonah spent three days buried under water. Lazarus spent three days in a grave. And Jesus was dead for three days, too, before he came back to life. Perhaps the ancient people of faith had a much more honest approach to and perspective on the human experience than we allow ourselves to have today.

The Outlaw is not a dark figure who threatens society. He or she is the restless one who is on a journey to discover something new about himself or herself—and his or her Creator. It is our acceptance, adoption, and willingness to divert any and all divine plans that will lead us right into the middle of it.

We spend too much time thinking about how others view us when we should be spending more time reflecting on how we view the world around us. Being misunderstood, out of place, and uncertain are not the characteristics of failure or suggestions of any premonition of destruction. They are the very urgings God uses to move us along our journey.

Death of a Soul

The day I discovered there was a letter being passed around among a small group of noisy church members (the folks who were dissatisfied with my leadership in youth ministry while I was in college) who needed someone to focus their frustration on, I felt vulnerable. And I didn't like it. A part of me started to die that day. And I've never been the same since.

I did the only thing I knew to do. I left my faith behind. If this is what it meant to follow God, then I was done. It would be almost five years before I would heal from that experience. That felt like an eternity for me.

During that time, I placed my faith in books and the intellectual pursuit of trying to piece together the broken pieces of my faith. I spent most of that time angry. So angry, in fact, that I didn't want to have anything to do with the things that I was supposed to care about so deeply—even God.

I took up running as a hobby. I ran forty to fifty miles a week. I would run as often as I could and even worked up enough courage to run a marathon. It helped pass the time and provided a great diversion from the pain inside. (I was also in the best shape of my life.)

Now that I look back on my obsession with running, I realize running was an external reality of my inward experience. I was running spiritually too. I didn't care where I was going. I just wanted it to be anywhere but the places that were the most familiar and the most painful.

The Great Surprise

Change is chaotic. It is painful. And few people will understand what is happening within you. My wife tried to understand and wanted to help. But I wasn't in any position to listen. It was a very lonely experience.

When you take on the role of Outlaw, most of the people in your life won't understand, and they may even feel threatened. That's to be expected. But the Outlaw eventually becomes the hero. Just like Jonah spent time digesting in the belly of a whale, the path of the Outlaw will take us into a digestive phase called transformation. We will emerge a different person—a Hero. We will eventually be welcomed back and championed by the very people who didn't understand why we were changing in the first place.

Not on Your Terms

The spiritual life is neither comfortable nor convenient. It does not play on your terms, but its own. You do not get to decide when, where, or how. Those things will be chosen for you. All you are responsible for saying is yes.

I don't know if this is true for you, but I've benefited a lot from mentors in my life. A few have lasted for a long time. These are people who I've stumbled upon and connected with in some meaningful way.

Some of them are very different from me. Some are similar. But each leader has played a significant role and offered me something of value that helped me through a difficult moment. They have been the voice of God at times, and they have been held me accountable for my decisions.

One of those mentors told me something I have never forgotten. I've acted on this numerous times, so much so that I am now confident enough in its truth that I am sharing it with others.

He told me, "Always say yes. You won't know if you need to say no until you are in the middle of it." He wasn't talking about opening myself up to destructive habits or criminal and unethical behavior. He meant that when you are given an opportunity for adventure, say yes.

It's impossible to have clarity moving forward. We want it so bad. And we're willing to trade the development of our souls for the illusion of predictability. It is a temptation that comes at too steep a price. The best chance we have at accomplishing something meaningful in life is to say yes and see what happens next.

The Outlaw separates himself or herself from the community because he or she no longer wants to be limited by predetermined standards. The Outlaw needs space to explore, reach, and live into his or her own curiosity. That doesn't mean the Outlaw doesn't have respect for order. It simply describes the process we must endure to internalize and own the permissions systems that will allow us to become the best expression of the individual breathed into us at the moment of our creation.

I remember a dream I had during this phase of wandering. I was walking toward a gothic-style church. I turned the corner and saw these stone steps leading up to two larger-than-life, dark wooden doors. They were closed. But I felt something within me tell me to go in anyway. I wasn't sure whether the doors would open, but they did. And when I got inside, I felt like I had arrived at home. It was comfortable and familiar, as if I had been there a hundred times before—only I knew for sure I had never been in this church before.

When I woke up the next morning, the dream stayed with me. I went to work as if it were just another day. About midday, I heard bells ringing from a nearby church. I decided to go and check it out. I wasn't sure why, but the dream still felt very real to me, even though I wasn't dreaming anymore.

As I turned the corner at the end of the block, I was standing in front of the same church I had seen in my dream. I had never paid any attention to it before. The doors were the same, only these doors were open, and there were a lot of people pouring into the church as if they had planned to be there for some specific event.

When I walked in, I had the same feeling of home and comfort that I had experienced in my dream. I looked down at the worship schedule I was handed as I walked into the church, and on the cover it read, "Ash Wednesday."

I was raised a good Southern Baptist. I had been taught that Ash Wednesday was for Catholics and that Catholics might not even be real Christians. But in that moment I knew I had made it through the desert and was ready for a new transition and pivot. I was ready to come back to myself—and to God. Only this time, the pieces would be put back together again in a very different order.

I will never forget the first time I heard these words read aloud:

Almighty and everlasting God, you hate nothing you have made and forgive the sins of all who are penitent: Create and make in us new and contrite hearts, that we, worthily lamenting our sins and acknowledging our wretchedness, may obtain of you, the God of all mercy, perfect remission and forgiveness; through Jesus Christ our Lord, who lives and reigns with you and the Holy Spirit, one God, for ever and ever. *Amen.*[1]

There was perhaps no more appropriate experience for me than to participate in the suffering of Christ by having ashes marked on my forehead. The whole thing felt strangely normal and yet full of meaning. I knew this would be the place where I would be brought back to life with respect to my spiritual journey.

The Point of No Return

Psychologists tell us that there is a moment in our decision making called the point of no return. It is the place where we have made up our minds, and no external or internal interference will keep us from acting on what we believe to be true.

I think this is true in the spiritual life as well. As we lean into the Outlaw, we will find there is a point of no return we experience right before we begin the phase of transformation.

Each time we step forward, we find the next step reveals something new about ourselves. And that insight shapes the way we view God, the people we love, and the people who love us. And it also shapes the way we see the world around us.

The Outlaw experience is not predefined or something that can be manufactured. It is an experience that will be known perfectly only by the person on the journey. I believe that was the way it was intended. And we have plenty of "desert" stories in the Christian tradition to substantiate that idea.

The paradox is that the desert is the place we go to escape God, but it is also the place we go to find God. Sometimes that desert is a literal wasteland. Sometimes it is the belly of the whale. Whichever path your journey takes you on, it is the misfits who seem to find it first and who are bold enough to push themselves to the brink of transformation. Or as I like to refer to it, the point of no return.

This was a point of no return for me. I knew I was entering a new phase. There was no way for me to go back, but I was ready to be spit back onto the shore like Jonah, so I could move forward.

Change is a chief characteristic of the spiritual life. If we do not change over time, we cannot be sure we are truly alive. The Creator left a life force within us at the moment of creation that gives us the urge to create as well. This life force isn't reserved for so-called creatives but for everyone. That means you. And people who create things understand that new things are rarely made out of something that doesn't exist. It is more accurately represented as the shaping of what already exists.

You are already being formed. You may not recognize it. You may deny it. But you are being shaped even as you read the words on this page. An evolution is taking place. The end result will be someone who is much closer in line with the intentions and motives of the Creator.

If you are on the outside, take comfort. That's exactly where you'll find the meaning you are looking for so that you will be ready for the transformation as it begins to take place in your life.

Chapter Four in Review

To Reflect On

- The harder we try to run away from something, the more likely that we'll run right into it.
- The Outlaw is not a dark figure who threatens society; he or she is the restless one who is on a journey to discover something new about himself or herself—and his or her Creator.
- Being misunderstood, out of place, and uncertain are not the characteristics of failure or suggestions of any premonition of destruction; they are the very urgings God uses to move us along our journey.
- Change is chaotic and painful.
- The Outlaw will eventually become the Hero.
- Before any transformation takes place, we must run and not look back.
- The spiritual life is neither comfortable nor convenient.
- Always say yes. You won't know if you need to say no until you are in the middle of it.
- It's impossible to have clarity moving forward.
- Separation describes the process we must endure to internalize and own the permissions systems that will allow us to become the best expression of the individual breathed into us at the moment of our creation.

- Choosing to become an Outlaw and separate yourself from what is normal and comfortable certainly marks a point of no return.
- Each time we step forward, we find the next step reveals something new about ourselves.
- The paradox is the desert is the place we go to escape God, but it is also the place we go to find God.
- Whichever path your journey takes you on, it is the misfits who seem to find it first and who are bold enough to allow push themselves to the brink of transformation.
- If we do not change over time, we cannot be sure we are truly alive.

To Ponder and Discuss

- Describe a time when you felt like you were running from something. What was going on in your life? What did you learn about yourself?
- Why is change so overwhelming? Why do we work so hard to resist it?
- Do you agree with the statement, "Always say yes"? Why or why not?
- Why is it that when we attempt to run fast and far away, we end up meeting God face to face?
- Are you or someone you know facing a "point of no return" moment? What is holding you back from letting go and moving forward?

PART TWO

The Magician

The greatest experience we will ever have is opening ourselves to change. Nothing that is fully alive remains the same. Life—absent of transformation—is nothing more than a continuation of someone else's hopes and dreams.

CHAPTER FIVE

That Which Stays the Same Is Always Changing

Finding God in our own stories is the beginning of our task.

—Carol Ochs

It's amazing to think about all that babies learn to do in the first two years of life. They learn to walk and then run. They learn how to talk—and talk some more. And they learn to drink from a bottle and later eat table food.

You could say that a baby's first two years of life on earth is nothing less than a perpetual state of change. Yet the little child is not even aware that what he or she is experiencing is not normal. In fact, it is the only normal he or she knows. (Maybe this is what Jesus was hinting at when he said the kingdom of God is available to those who come as a little child.)

The speed at which life changes is unrecognizable until we get older and become more aware of ourselves, others, and the circumstances in which we find ourselves. It becomes even clearer as you watch others—especially your children—grow up right before your very eyes. Raising children is a magnificent process full of frustration, hope, excitement, and a-ha moments that are worthy of an infinite number of pictures—and a little bit of chocolate, too.

But children are unpredictable. And so is the journey to starting a family. Brooke and I thought starting a family would be easy for us, but it was not. In fact, both of our boys gave us a good scare before they even entered the world.

A Not-So-Good Friday

We received a call from the doctor who was interested in running more tests based on some not-so-normal results from Brooke's latest lab work. Up to that point, everything seemed normal. (Not that there is anything normal about a human being growing inside of you.) We were enjoying the moment and beginning to plan and prepare for what was about to happen next. The worst part was that it would be two weeks before we could get in to see the specialists we needed to see.

We were enjoying the excitement of being young and expecting our first child. I was preparing for my first marathon. Brooke was getting our home ready for our first child. We were so young and naive. It never occurred to us that anything bad might happen.

We had tried for over a year to get pregnant. It was a big deal when it finally happened. As most first-time, soon-to-be parents react, we started planning the baby's life and carefully preparing ourselves in great detail to welcome this new life into the world.

So when we received the call from the doctor who suggested there was a chance something was wrong with our baby, we had no idea what to think, feel, or say. Neither of us had any idea something like this might actually happen. Our excitement turned to fear. Our perfect bubble was burst.

It might have been Good Friday on the calendar, but there was nothing good about it. I still remember crossing the starting line of my first marathon and wondering if my son would be able to run a marathon with me one day. It was enough to make my heart drop into my stomach and my eyes become blurred from the water welling up in my eyes.

When Carter was finally born and was perfectly healthy with ten fingers and ten toes, we both took a deep breath, though I suspect Brooke's deep breath was probably a little deeper than mine. She had been a lot more involved in the process. Hearing our son scream for the first time was a beautiful sound.

There is something magical about the birth of a child. How can something come from nothing? How do two people create something new? I'm certainly not in need of a biology lesson. But I can think of few other things in life that come with such wonder and amazement.

Life Is Change

A woman giving birth is a theme we see through most ancient literature, including the Bible. Every time a birth happens, there is a great deal of meaning surrounding the event. It is the beginning of something new, and nothing is the same again. So birth is a perfect metaphor to explore the transformation of the soul and the new things that result from that transformation.

The Outlaw within us clears the way for the transformation process to begin. The Outlaw forces us to remove all the obstacles within us that will hinder our journey through the process or change. It is necessary that we become the Outlaw; otherwise, we will not have the strength to endure the power and force of the Magician.

The Outlaw is disruptive, uncomfortable, and confrontational. We must come into direct opposition with the things that might prevent us from moving forward. It is in doing so that we will find the courage to push through the overwhelming sense of change we'll experience in the midst of transformation.

When we are ready to let go of the illusions we cling to today so we are ready to reach forward to what is next for us, we activate the Magician within us. It is the Magician who possesses the power to change. And change is the only state of being the Magician knows. Like a child—or his or her parents—nothing stays the same long. Life—for the Magician—is in a constant state of adaptation.

Charles Darwin's thought can be summarized in the words, "It is not the most intellectual of the species that survives; it is not the strongest that survives; but the species that survives is the one that is able to adapt to and to adjust best to the changing environment in which it finds itself."[1] The scariest parts of ourselves are not those parts we can't control but those we refuse to change. It places artificial barriers to our success and fulfillment that were intended for our enjoyment, satisfaction, and fulfillment.

Opposites Attract

When most of us think about magicians, we think about the people we often see on stage doing card tricks or any variety of impossible things, like slicing someone in two and then putting them back together again. That type of magician is meant to entertain, but this is far from its classical posture.

Sometimes magicians are thought to be witches and characters associated with dark magic meant to control or harm others. Magicians are denounced by some faith groups and misunderstood by others. But this is to be expected. Transformation is not a process we can quantify or dissect. It looks and feels different for every person. And the path to and through transformation is unique to who we are and who we are meant to become.

Transformation is not pretty, safe, or predictable. Rightly so, transformation will come with both darkness and light, both celebration and defeat, both fear and joy. The surprise will come in our realization that two opposites can coexist. In fact, it is the tension of those two forces that creates the friction we need to guide our steps through transformation.

The truth is that light exists in darkness. Hope exists in despair. And life exists within death.

Most of the Western world has been preoccupied with separating things and compartmentalizing them. We want to understand how everything works, pull everything apart, and give a label to each part. If we can provide a label, then we'll know what to do with something.

The only flaw in that perspective is that it assumes all the variables will remain the same. But my experience has taught me that which stays the same is always changing. Magic is not about the power of dark things but about seeing the interconnectedness of all things and finding yourself in the changing shapes all around you.

A False Sense of Security

Security built around our ability to dissect and document every aspect of life (or God for that matter) will always fall short. There is no security in attempting to know all things unless you have the potential to know all things. And just to be clear: you don't have the power to do so. It's impossible. Every construct we apply to God, by default, limits the person of God. By definition, a god with limits wouldn't be God.

If it's impossible to know everything, then we must find a new source of our security. What we will discover is that the only true place of security is getting comfortable with the process of change and transformation. The variables of life are constantly moving—faster than we can catalog and reference. Some of what you do today and consider normal didn't exist five years ago. Some of what you will be doing in five years (and will consider normal) has yet to be invented.

That is the speed at which we are moving through this life. So perhaps we can learn from our children, who don't see anything wrong with change until they learn from us that change is something to be resisted and rejected until there is no other option.

As we move from the Outlaw to the Magician, we must allow another part of ourselves to be activated. This will position us to move through the trials and tribulations that we will confront. These exist not to trip us up as much as to mold and shape us so we will be ready for what's ahead of us.

The Currency of Transformation

The desert experience is not something that is foreign to the Christian traditions—or other traditions of that matter. The children of Israel left Egypt and wandered in the desert for four decades before they entered the land promised to them by God. Jesus went into the desert for forty days and faced a series of temptations before he began his public ministry. And John was imprisoned on a island for the remainder of his life where he worked out his own spiritual stories.

Isolation. Silence. Pain. Joy. Dreams. Darkness. These are the currencies that spend in the economy of transformation. There is no other path for living into what was divinely breathed into us at the moment of our creation other than through the desert. It is our only option. And it is not a place that we will pass through only once, but again and again.

Transformation takes us from where we are today to a new place. The door behind us is closed. Our only option is to move forward. And this is the role of the Magician.

The Gospels also record a time when Jesus took on his heavenly form. He took his trusted three disciples—Peter, James, and John—to the top of the mountain. If a spiritual leader ever asks you to go to the top of a mountain, you can rest assured you will experience something only you will understand. And it will likely be something that will scare you to death yet provide all the confirmation you need about the substance of that leader—all in the same moment.

It was at the top of this mountain where the three disciples saw something they could neither explain nor deny. Jesus took on a different shape. He became the embodiment of the heavenly kingdom he talked so much about. They were terrified, as the story goes, until a voice from heaven approved the work of Jesus.

It is good to know that even the people who walked and talked with the Messiah on earth were terrified. It gives me a sense of hope that my general hesitation toward transformation is a time-honored tradition passed down from those who came before me. If they can be terrified yet comforted at the same time, then why should I expect my experience of transformation to be much different?

Perspective Matters

I once dreamed I was in a school classroom. I was by myself and busy doing something. I was only by myself for a short time. It wasn't long before another person walked into the room. I wasn't sure who he was, but he seemed like he had as much right to be in the classroom as I did. He didn't make me nervous, but it was only the two of us. We had a conversation about something, but I wasn't sure what.

All of a sudden the intensity in the room changed. In an instant, the other boy was lifted off the ground and changed shape into what I knew in my gut was the devil. His skin changed, his eyes rolled back into his head, and his voice changed.

This transformed being told me to stop going down this path. Stop heading in the direction I was heading or bad things would happen to me. I was scared.

The path to which he was referring was unclear to me, but his insistence that I not proceed any farther was clear. Soon the devil-ish character transformed back into human form and left the room. I remember feeling as if my breath had been taken away.

My first instinct was to think this was a message of resistance from an outside force of evil. As I have thought about that dream over time, I'm more and more convinced that I was talking to myself. My fear and anxiety about what was ahead for me were troubling me more than what my conscious mind allowed me to process.

Fear is powerful and has the ability to influence our thinking and our behavior. Fear is often associated with objects and ideas such as evil and darkness. These things come with cultural and religious baggage. But one of the greatest demons we will ever have to face is the part of ourselves that refuses to let go of the illusions of certainty. This part of us wants to do everything within its power to cling to what is passing away and prevent us from reaching for what will be.

Often the devil—the enemy—we have to fear is not "out there" but within our minds. The greatest obstacle to transformation is not your situation or your circumstances. It's not your age, education, or family. It is you.

The Magician possesses the power to transform one object into something else. If you are the Magician, then you have the power to allow yourself to be changed. But it is only you who can make that decision.

Only you keep you from becoming the person you were divinely inspired to become. The greatest obstacle to your progress is you. You must give yourself permission to change, or you never will.

Expect the Unexpected

I once met with a woman who was dying from a variety of complications. She was in the intensive care unit and not predicted to leave the hospital alive. She was among the few ninety-year-olds I'd ever met who had as much technical acumen as I did. She had to. Her family was scattered all over the world. It was the only way she could stay in touch with them.

One particular afternoon, she told me a dream she had the night before. You never quite knew what was going to happen when she said something like that. Needless to say, she had my full attention.

She said she dreamed she had died and had gone to hell. She looked around and wondered where she was. Eventually, she met face to face with the Devil himself. They had a conversation. He then told her, "I don't know what do with you. We don't want you. Go back home."

That may sound bizarre to some people, but I couldn't help myself from laughing. And she did, too. It was a great comic relief for her in the midst of some very painful circumstances.

Most people spend their lives in fear of the devil, especially fear of not escaping him after death. Her experience was entirely different. He didn't know what to with her, so he sent her back. Knowing this woman, I would say his assessment was right.

She was a bright spirit but a spitfire in every way. I imagine she raised plenty of hell in her time on earth, but I know she did a tremendous amount of good, too. I'll never forget her—or that moment she shared in the hospital room.

Isn't it funny how our perspective on things can change over time? There was a time in her life when she feared the devil. But now, in the face of death, she had no fear. This is what we can expect as we live into a state of normalcy where that which stays the same is always changing.

Opening ourselves to power of the Magician to transform our lives will leave us different and change our outlook on life. The lens through which we interpret the world around us will change over time. It is our job to keep saying yes—even when it scares us. It is the only way we'll ever realize that what seems scary is really the brilliance breathed within us that has yet to be realized.

We want things to stay the same because we can presume to exert control over them. Transformation begins with letting go and facing life with eyes wide open. It's scary, but only for a moment. Then we realize it is the breath of fresh air we've needed for far too long.

Chapter Five in Review

To Reflect On

- Every time a birth happens or new life begins, there is a great deal of meaning surrounding that event.
- It is necessary that we become the Outlaw; otherwise, we will not have the strength to endure the power and force of the Magician.
- We must let go of the illusions we cling to today so we can reach forward to what is next.
- The scariest parts of ourselves are not those parts we can't control but those we refuse to change.
- Transformation is not pretty, safe, or predictable.
- It is the tension of two conflicting forces that creates the friction we need to guide our steps through transformation.
- Magic is not about the power of dark things but about seeing the interconnectedness of all things and finding yourself in the changing shapes all around you.
- Security built around our ability to dissect and document every aspect of life (or God for that matter) will always fall short.
- Isolation. Silence. Pain. Joy. Dreams. Darkness. These are the currencies that spend in the economy of transformation.
- The greatest devil we will ever have to face is the part of ourselves that refuses to let go of the illusions of certainty.
- It is our job to keep saying yes—even when it scares us.

- Confidence in things that stay the same is the antithesis of faith.
- Transformation begins with letting go and facing life with eyes wide open.

To Ponder and Discuss

- Define transformation. What is it? What is it not?
- Remember a time in your life when you experienced new life. What happened? What did you learn about yourself?
- Why do we exert so much energy resisting change? Why is it that the things that last forever adapt over time (for example, love, grace, forgiveness, and so on)?
- List three things that are holding you back from living the life you were meant to live. How can you use those hindrances to help you move forward?
- How does perspective influence your decisions? What perspectives need to change in your life?

The Illusions That Captivate

My dear fellow, who will let you?
That's not the point. The point is, who will stop me?

—Ayn Rand[1]

The bells of the church on the end of the block would ring at noon every day. I'm sure they rang at other times, but that was when I heard them. The first time I heard the bells, I ended up at the church I had seen in my dream and in the midst of my first Ash Wednesday service. That was the beginning of something I couldn't even fully understand at the time.

Before I left the Ash Wednesday service that day, I realized there was a midday Eucharist service held every day at the cathedral. It was just about one city block from my office downtown. Just as I had felt compelled to come to the church in the first place, I felt compelled to come back.

So the very next day I returned. I went to a few doors in order to find the one that opened. Being a downtown church, I had to press a button and wait for a nice, pleasant voice to allow me to enter. When I did, I had no idea where to go.

The very helpful receptionist pointed me down the hall and to the right. It was there that I found a small chapel room just off the main sanctuary. Clearly the atmosphere was much more sublime than it had been the day before. The simplicity of the chapel was such that it offered very little distraction and provided a perfect place to focus on the holy, which is always around us but which we are not very good at being aware of.

The candles lit in rows, the altar, the different crosses, and even the prayer book were new and different. I felt like a fish out of water because nothing seemed familiar. I had no idea what was about to happen, nor did I know what I was expected to do. And yet the desire to know and experience was what kept me from bolting out and sneaking back to the office.

As I sat in a silence, about a half dozen other people seemed to have heard the church bells, too. They were more familiar with the place and acknowledged each other through the way their eyes connected, but without speaking a word. They had been there before.

There were only a few rows of chair set up before the altar. I made sure to grab a seat in the very back, not because it was crowded but because this is where I had the viewpoint I needed to follow the lead of others. As the priest entered the room, we stood. I didn't know why, but we did. The order of events was new to me, so I felt slightly behind the rest of the people in the room in just about everything. I'm sure I was the only one who noticed, but I felt like I had a sign on my forehead that read "New Guy!"

I had been in church most of my life. My mom even says that I was in church nine months before I was born. But this experience was very different from the church I grew up in. If I weren't willing to be open to what was different, then I never would have realized the new life I experienced in that room over time.

I was beginning again. Everything was new. I was full of questions, wonder, and amazement. I had worked so hard to run away from my faith and God that I had started to miss that side of myself. It's like getting mad at your friend in elementary school in the morning but forgetting why you were mad by lunch. And by recess you were playing together as if nothing had happened.

It wasn't quite as clean as that. The stinging reality of what had happened was still very clear. I knew I had lost my way, and my hope and desire was to find a new practice and a new vocabulary so I might be able to put the pieces back together again.

When it was time to take the elements, everyone went forward. All six of us kneeled at the prayer rail and waited for the priest to place the wafer in our hands and to offer us the wine in the cup. As I consumed both, something happened within me. It was as if I had been there a thousand times, and it felt like a thousand people were in the room cheering me on. It was one of those holy moments you never forget but fear sharing for the strange looks you might receive from others.

I never knew who was going to be at one of these midday Eucharist services, yet it didn't really matter. The more I went, the more I began to recognize their faces, though none of us felt compelled to know each others' names or swap vCards and contact information. We were just happy to see each other and pass the peace.

I also never knew who I was going to kneel next to. It was not unusual to have a homeless man on one side and a businessman in a custom-tailored suit on the other. It seemed strange, yet at the same time it seemed as if it was the perfect mix. There was no obstacle, no prerequisite to come and kneel and celebrate brokenness and redemption together.

Everyone had rightful access to God, no matter what events had led them there. For a brief moment, I could imagine in my mind the intersection of the past, present, and future. I suspect this is what the mystics meant when they talked about the communion of the saints.

Those midday services were small, likely financially unprofitable, and yet perfect in every way. I didn't even need to be a member of the church to participate. I was given a script to follow and a set of expected events to anticipate in proper order. My job was not to interpret or apply but to participate and be fully present in the moment.

This small, inconsequential (by most standards), and predictable recurring event would become for me the place where I found my faith again. It was the place where I started all over and experienced everything as if I were a beginner. Had my illusions of certainty surrounding practice and worship clouded my mind, I would never have opened myself up to realize that sacred things are everywhere and in everyone.

Open to New Things

The Magician knows we are in no better position to be transformed than when we are open to new things. It is so easy to grab
onto the things that are passing away with all our strength and
energy. It is a futile effort that will ultimately leave us holding onto
our past and inhibiting our ability to live into our future.

There are a variety of illusions that we desperately want to be
true in our lives. We want to know that the career we choose and
the education we completed will take us to new heights of success.
We want to know that the financial planning we participate in will
insulate us from market inconsistencies. We want to know that if we
send our children to private schools and provide the best for them,
they will somehow get a leg up on the process of climbing their own
ladder.

The reality is that most of our lives can't be controlled or contained by any plan. We can have all the power, position, and prestige
in the world and still not have the ability to prevent change or even
redirect the process by which we are formed—and transformed.

When the boss says, "Thank you for your service," what now?
When your child flunks out of his or her freshman year of college,
what now? When your financial planning didn't account for a few
unexpected twists and turns, what now? When your spouse is diag-
nosed with cancer, what now? When the people you consider your
spiritual leaders let you down, what now?

All of life is an illusion. The only certainty we can have is the
moments in which we are present. It is an opportunity we get sixty

times every minute to be fully present and own the life that is in us to breathe. We don't get just one chance to get it right; we get a seemingly infinite number of chances to get it right. But the things that we want to ensure our security and stability moving forward are, ironically, the same things that have the potential to hold us back.

Proving Others Wrong

I have lived most of my life doing things that other people thought I wouldn't be able to do. In high school, I was the smart kid from the wrong neighborhood. Maybe that's why I've spent most of my life trying to prove myself to others. Perhaps I'm still looking for their approval. It's embarrassing to think about. I've been out of high school for a long time, but some of those experiences and feelings still haunt me.

It is likely I am not the only one who is living to find approval in other people and institutions alike. We plan our educations, career paths, and family decisions to meet someone else's standards. We convince ourselves that these are in our best interests when, in reality, they are in *their* best interests. The illusion of approval and acceptance is one that has captivated and awestruck our modern culture. The latest cars, the biggest houses, the fanciest clothes, and the most extravagant vacations are fleeting and futile. There will always be someone who lures you to move just a little farther down that path to get what you want. It is a carrot that you'll never catch.

So we spend our lives searching and reaching for people, places, and opportunities that we are convinced will bring us true happiness. We say the right things, listen to the right people, and follow the rules. It all seems to work just fine until it doesn't. And then we don't know what to do other than hunker down and wait for things to return to the way they were so that we can get our lives back on track.

The only thing I am certain of is that spiritual formation does not take place from the outside in. We can only become the person that was breathed into us at the moment of our creation if we live from the inside out. And we are all guilty of falling prey to the whims and wishes of a society and culture—however holy or unholy—that promises something it can't give us: satisfaction and fulfillment.

Any human or institution will let you and me down eventually. And that funk will further push us away from opening ourselves to the transformation that needs to take place within. The promise the Magician makes us is that we can either be sidelined by the expectations of others or transformed through the opening of ourselves to new things.

More Than a Vocation

You and I were created for more than the roles that define us today. We were created to become our true selves. We were created because we have a unique gift to offer the world. The experiences we collect, the people we love, and lives that we live will either contain or reveal that gift. How sad a commentary it would be to leave this earth without ever really feeling alive.

The truth is, the reason why I think I am out on my own in an office I've built out back writing ten thousand words or so every week is not because I have been endowed to pursue a path somehow more pure than a banker on Wall Street. It is because I need a desert experience full of solitude, silence, and habit at each moment in time to make me come to grips with the illusions that seem to still captivate me and move me along this life.

Not a month goes by that I don't feel real fear about the choices I've made—*what if something goes terribly wrong with my writing career, and I can't support my family? Maybe we would have been better off if I'd stayed in an office job.* But moving in this direction has pushed me to the edge of what I know to be real and true. It scares me to death, but I keep pushing and keep moving forward—not because I am certain about the twists and turns but because I believe it is shaping me into the person I was intended to be.

The Wonder of Transformation

My decision to go out on my own seemed like an absolutely ridiculous idea to most people I knew. I couldn't even anticipate what would happen next. And I was fully aware there was a great possibility of failure. But I was tired of being told no. I resisted the artificial boundaries that were put in front of me. If I could generate millions of dollars in revenue for someone else, why couldn't I do that for myself? Yes, it might fail, but what if it didn't? What if it worked? What if I stumbled into something that allowed me to follow my passion and do the things that really light me up inside?

I refused to accept that any company was going to take care of me. That was an illusion I had seen broken before me time and time again. I refused to believe that I couldn't work harder than anyone else and show up to the table to play more than anyone else. I refused to believe that corporate benefits were worth exchanging more than four decades of my life to have. I refused to believe that the world wasn't changing and what I was sure of today would not shift tomorrow.

The greater risk in my mind was not jumping out on my own; the greater risk was staying captive to a perspective that said that if I just sat down, shut up, and waited my turn, someone else would come along and grant me permission to be me. Forget that! No thanks!

When I decided to leave my job, I was married and had one young son. It was 2009—the height of the Great Recession. I was told I was too young, too inexperienced, and it was the wrong time to be doing this. I was told I wouldn't make it and would come crawling back for my job.

The first ninety days of entrepreneurship scared me to death. For the first time, I had to live with my hands open—just like I had to kneel and accept the elements from the priest during every midday Eucharist service. It was a posture that I was not too comfortable taking, but one that I knew possessed a power I had not yet released in my life—the power of letting go of one thing so I could reach forward for something greater.

And it was when I was about to the end of what I knew was possible that things started to shift. Momentum started to build. And I found a new order and cadence to life. I needed a miracle to happen, and it did.

Unexpected Surprises

Shortly after I announced my resignation, Brooke and I found out we were expecting our second child. Perhaps this should have made me rethink my decision to start my own business. But something about the miracle of Brooke getting pregnant again was the confirmation I needed that the impossible was possible. And it was a miracle.

If we thought getting pregnant the first time was difficult, the second time was even harder. Brooke had to have two surgeries to remove a growth around her uterus that was inhibiting her ability to get pregnant. But we didn't discover that at first. We tried for two years. We went to fertility clinics to be tested.

We knew we wanted another child, and we weren't going to take no for an answer. If we couldn't make that happen biologically, then we would find another way. Some people might have given up and given in. Not us. We wanted the end result more than we were tied to a particular process or path. And just as we were beginning to explore adoption agencies so we could expand our family, we were blessed with a new life.

If we ever hope to experience life in all its fullness and abundance, we can't give up. Even when we want to, we must keep pushing forward. Change is hard, and transformation is uncomfortable. But it is the only path by which we shed that which holds us back and take that part of us we have yet to discover.

Focus Determines Direction

I think losing focus on what really matters—what lasts forever—is the great temptation we must face as we release the illusions we hold close to us. If we don't have a clear picture of what's ahead, then we cling to what we think is secure today. There is a part of the human experience that needs a sense of normal. And if one isn't provided for us, we'll create it ourselves.

But there is also a paradox hidden within the desire to see what is ahead. In short, we can't. If we could, then life would be absent of faith. And faith is required to respond to our call to constant transformation and our pursuit of what we have yet to fully understand. In lieu of certainty, we accept that transformation is a process that we can count on. As we move through the process (not once but a lifetime of personal evolution) we realize that any sense of a destination is an arrival, too. The only secure and stable thing we can ever hope to possess in this life is change.

Our pursuit of financial independence may mean choosing a path that leads to exceptional wealth. It also may mean choosing a path that requires very little money to live and survive. Our pursuit of physical fitness and personal health may mean choosing to assemble a personal staff of dietitians, trainers, and doctors. It also may mean choosing a path that relies on raw foods, a low-stress lifestyle, and general weight control. Our pursuit of having children may mean procreation. It also may mean foster care or adoption.

There is more than one way to get to the same point. If that is the case, then we can't accept the limits or boundaries other people place upon. Even if those people act with good intentions.

When we give ourselves permission to pursue transformation, we must also release ourselves from the things we are certain of. If we don't, then our illusions will captivate us and inhibit our ability to continue on in the journey and complete the adventure that is before us. The Magician must have permission to do the work within us that we have yet to admit needs to be done.

Opposites Attract

The gift we have from our Creator to pursue this path of transformation is faith. It is the compass that God placed within us to direct our steps. There is no clear path—only hints—at how to discern that which has yet to be seen. This is why we consume the elements during the Eucharist. It is only when we consume life as it is and as we are that we can digest the truth about ourselves and the world around us.

Faith invites us to bring into harmony two often-opposing forces: the inner world and the outer world. Both are riddled with illusions of certainty and doubt. What we will come to realize over time is that both are two parts of one thing: the fulfilled life. And a fulfilled life is one full of taking in and letting go. It is the only hope we have to become the person buried beneath the expectations of others and the illusions of certainty cluttering our hearts, minds, and perspective.

Chapter Six in Review

To Reflect On

- We are in no better position to be transformed than when we are open to new things.
- We can have all the power, position, and prestige in the world and still not have the ability to prevent change or even redirect the process by which we are formed—and transformed.
- All of life is an illusion.
- The things that we want to ensure our security and stability moving forward are, ironically, the same things that have the potential to hold us back.
- The illusion of approval and acceptance is one that has captivated and awestruck our modern culture.
- It all seems to work just fine until it doesn't.
- We can only become the person that was breathed into us at the moment of our creation if we live from the inside out.
- Becoming our true self is not a vocational question, because God didn't create us for a vocation.
- You and I were created for more than the roles that define us today.
- The experiences we collect, the people we love, and lives that we live will either contain or reveal that gift that we have uniquely been given to share with the world.
- Change is hard, and transformation is uncomfortable.

- Losing focus on what really matters—what lasts forever—is the great temptation we must face as we release the illusions we hold close to us.
- The only secure and stable thing we can ever hope to possess in this life is change.
- When we give ourselves permission to pursue transformation, we must also release ourselves from the things of which we are certain.
- There is no clear path—only hints—at how to discern that which has yet to be seen.
- Faith demands that we bring into harmony two often-opposing forces: the inner world and the outer world.

To Ponder and Discuss

- Why is adventure what we talk about but certainty is what we pursue? Should it be the other way around? Why or why not?
- What role does faith play in personal transformation?
- What powers your internal compass? Why do you do what you do? Who do you do it for?
- Think of a time when you did all the right things, but the situation didn't work out like you had hoped. What happened? What did you learn about yourself?
- Are you living life from the outside in or the inside out? Why does it matter?

CHAPTER SEVEN

Finding Courage in Destruction

The mystery is this: There is one right thing to do at every moment. We can either follow or resist.

—Robert Johnson

I was on a plane from Houston to Nashville my senior year of high school. My goal was to visit two colleges while visiting a friend. I had been flying all my life, so nothing about the process was new or unfamiliar to me. I arrived at my gate and boarded the plane shortly thereafter.

We taxied from the gate toward the runway. Only we didn't make it. We came to a stop and stayed there long enough for most of us on the plane that Friday afternoon to know something wasn't right.

And sure enough, about thirty minutes later we were headed back to the gate.

The very polite staff asked us to get off the plane while we waited for an alternate one to arrive. It was some type of mechanical trouble, but I can't remember the exact reason. I was not upset because this was not my first time enduring this exercise. And flying was less formal pre-9/11.

I sat down next to a random guy. He was about six feet tall, wore sleek glasses, and had on a black suit. His tie was ever so slightly loosened and top button undone. But he still looked very professional. We made some small talk. I asked him where he was headed once we got to Nashville. He indicated that Nashville was home.

Being naturally curious, I asked him what he did for a living. He handed me his business card and said he was an admissions officer for Belmont University. I'm sure the look on my face gave away my surprise.

I explained that Belmont was one of the two schools I hoped to visit while in Nashville. We talked about Nashville and Belmont for about an hour before it was time to board the flight.

As we were gathering our things, we realized that we'd both miss each other based on when I had my admissions appointment. He did know the person I would be meeting with and said he'd put in a good word. He was going to be in the office that following Monday, only a short while before he headed back onto the road.

We both said our goodbyes and shook our heads at the odds of our meeting in Houston. It seemed so random, yet it seemed too planned.

When I arrived on campus for my interview, I was astonished once again when the same guy I had met in the airport came out to call me back from my interview. I think we were both as surprised to see each other. He explained that when he got back in the office his travel plans had changed. He wasn't leaving until the day after he was originally scheduled to leave.

I think we all have those moments where we secretly wonder if someone or something else is controlling the universe. Both encounters could not have been humanly planned or orchestrated. The fact they took place gave me enough reason to pay attention.

Subtle Cues and Slender Threads

The arrival of the Magician in our lives is probably much more subtle than we anticipate. Many people are waiting for Merlin the Magician to show up in a strange outfit and pointy stick. But the magic the Magician releases in our lives when we are open to change is through the slender threads that connect one event to the next, one relationship to the next. There are times when there seems to be an infinite number of options to choose from, so many options it seems paralyzing.

Don't believe me? Try shopping for cereal for the kids at the grocery story. If you let them choose, you'll have an entire cart of just cereal. There are so many options that it's impossible to settle only on one or two boxes. The anxiety involved in choosing the right cereal with the right toy is enough to make any parent need a nap.

But then there are times when the next step seems so obvious it just can't be true. The most common context for this idea is when you meet the man or woman of your dreams. I did. And I'm not just saying that because I need to make up for my shortfalls with the woman who decided to spend her life with me. Even if I were, I'm not convinced there are enough sentences and paragraphs to make up for all my shortfalls.

Meeting her was magical. The Greeks believed that a *nous* (or soul) was separated at the beginning of time. The search for companionship was the eternal longing to find your other half. And when you did, it was as if you both knew and recognized each other, even if it was the first time you had met. Something inside you just jumped and felt as if you'd known that person your whole life.

The only problem was that I was a bachelor kind of guy at the time. I prided myself on resisting attachment to any relationship. I didn't want to be tied down. I wanted to keep my options opened. I even developed a quota system for myself in college. I needed to go out with at least three girls a minimum of three times each to consider the semester complete.

But one night I had a dream. I was at a performance of some kind. I couldn't see anybody's face in the dream. Even though I could only see from the knee down, I could hear myself having conversations with other people. So I don't think I was looking down or trying to avoid anyone.

Then I felt this person come toward me wearing a Renaissance-styled dress. We spoke to each other, and I felt myself jump inside. It was as if I had found my other half.

When I woke up, I told my roommate about my dream. I told him that I believed I was going to meet the person I would marry sometime in the very near future. He rolled his eyes and grunted. I don't think he was quite as convinced as I was about the truth of the dream. He was more interested in borrowing my shaving cream and the leftovers in the fridge.

A few months into dating Brooke, the dream was confirmed, and I realized she was the one. I attended a madrigal dinner she was performing in for her university. When she came over to the table where I was sitting with her family, I briefly looked down and realized I had seen that same dress in my dream. Once again, I felt something jump inside and knew the pieces of life were being assembled in such a way that I couldn't anticipate and also couldn't resist.

How did I know? I can't really explain it. But I was convinced in that moment that she was the part of me I had unknowingly been searching for all along. I didn't share this realization with her immediately—just because something strikes you as profound doesn't mean it needs to be immediately shared, but saved for the right time and context.

Finding Alignment

All of us have those moments where we feel like everything in the universe aligned at the right time, or where we understand God has made something real or visible. I am not a golfer, but I am told that it only takes one good hit to get you to come back to golf again.

This is also true as we develop and live into becoming the people we we destined to become at the moment of our creation. It is the small things that we only connect one at a time that later, looking back, become a chain of events that clearly led to where we are today.

But no matter where you are today, you were not designed to stay there. You might be at the pinnacle of your success, but change is coming. You might be at the depths of depression: know that change is coming. You might be at best place in your marriage and relationships: know that change is coming.

It's easy to resist change because it is unfamiliar and uncomfortable. But unfamiliar and uncomfortable are the characteristics of transformation. If we reject those things and avoid them, the Magician will not have permission to work within us to bring us into alignment with our deepest desires.

What should be clear can quickly become so convoluted and confusing. This is why we need the Outlaw to disrupt our lives: we need to get rid of the layers and the noise that keep us from paying attention to the world around us.

Distracted from Ourselves

We live in a distracted age. There is very little time in our day when we are not connected or close to some type of device alerting us to any number of things and asking us to respond. If you're like most people, you have a smartphone, tablet, and a computer or laptop. It is likely that every person in your family does, too. We willingly inflict ourselves with the temptation to be anywhere but present within the moment. Yet being present is where we will find the courage and will to destroy the illusions that are holding us back so we are ready to reach into the process of being made new again.

Scientists are beginning to explore and research how the habit of people who feel compelled to stay connected and respond immediately to every alert on their various devices is similar to other addictions on the planet. The brain seems to fire and respond to these triggers in the same way. And the trouble with addicts who are not yet in recovery is that they are unaware of just how distorted they are and how disconnected they are from themselves.

What this means is that many of us are addicted to the illusion of connectedness with the world around us. The irony is that we can't connect with anyone or anything until we are grounded in an understanding of who we are. The process of transformation is not one that is so much about change within other people but how change within us contributes to the change that happens in the people and circumstances around us.

This is true whether you are an accountant for a top-five firm, a surgeon in worldwide demand, or a school teacher in rural America. It is true whether you are a dreamer or a pragmatist, whether you are a literalist or prefer to see shades of gray wherever you look.

The truth is, change affects us before it affects anyone else. But that change is rarely so profound and epic. That's why we miss it so many times. Unless we are paying attention, we'll never understand just how interconnected we are to seemingly disconnected realities.

I'm not suggesting you start sitting under a tree and meditating for hours at a time. I'm also not suggesting you seek out a traditional vision quest either. What I'm suggesting is that you find a way to disconnect from the distractions of life, clean out the junk, and lean into the transformation that will naturally happen as a result of that effort.

Selling the Spiritual Life

My first sales manager told me two things that I believe contain profound insight into the spiritual life. He said the longer you sell the same product, the less effective you are likely to be doing it. This seemed out of order to me. It seems only natural that you would get better at something the longer you do it.

He explained that the more familiar you are with any product or service, the less likely you are to ask good questions of others. Worse, you assume you already know the answer to a question that has yet to be asked.

The second thing he told me is that sales is not about being the smartest, most outgoing, or even the most skilled. It's about showing up and doing the work. He would regularly remind me that sales is ten percent luck and ninety percent perspiration. As it turned out, he was spot on.

Taking that out of a business context and looking at it through the lens of the spiritual life, we find that when we stop asking good questions, we limit—or even prohibit—the change that needs to take place in our lives. We start to get comfortable with the status quo. We hold fast to our routines and stop pursuing the process of being made new again and again. Slowly we drift into a place where we are so out of touch with the tension that rests within us that we don't have the energy or the time to waste on personal transformation.

Respond and Refocus

The call of the Magician is our opportunity to respond by refocusing our attention on the things that give us life—not just the things that make a life. It's easy to get so busy doing things that we forget why we do them in the first place. And until we lose our job, our marriage fails, or our kids are arrested, we don't wake up to what we've been trying to tell ourselves for far too long.

The connection between the world we see and the world we do not see is much more profound than we might first think. The Magician invites us through subtle moments and occurrences to wake up, pay attention, and observe just how interconnected life is. Our resistance to waking up is less about our inability to do so than it is our unwillingness to see things as they are.

But even more detrimental to our progress is that we stop showing up entirely. Before the Magician can do the work within us, we must be actively engaged in the process. We must follow the cues, respond to the urgings, and pursue our deepest desires. It is our curiosity and openness to the possibility that something closer to our true selves exists in front of us that keeps us moving forward.

Gurus and Gold

Robert Johnson talks about two concepts in his book *Balancing Heaven and Earth* that I believe are relevant to this phase of our journey. One I've already mentioned: the slender threads that link the world around us. Johnson encourages seekers to follow the slender threads because they will lead to places seekers want to go.

The second concept he discusses is allowing others to "hold your gold" for a period of time. He says you will meet people throughout life who will become mentors of sorts to you. For a period of time you give yourself to them so you can learn and grow. Then at an undetermined time, you will take you gold back and continue to move forward.

You might think you only take your gold back when a guru has done something wrong or led you down a wrong path, but Johnson recognizes something that even the ancients wrote about: there is a season for everything. No one person, circumstance, or construct is big enough to hold you and captivate you forever. The process of taking your gold back is a moment to be celebrated, not criticized. It signals that you've grown as much as you can and are ready to move forward.

I have been lucky enough to have people come and go in my life who have held my gold for me. Some of them are still holding some of my gold. But every one of them has taught me something. Through their story, I have found a way to back into mine.

Hinting at What Is to Come

What we learn about ourselves from others is a hint at what is to come if we are brave enough to continue along in our journey. Not only will we be shaped, but there will soon come a time when our story of transformation will inspire others to find their own strength to enter into a way of living that makes a chaotic culture full of change seem manageable.

If we do not find the courage in destroying and breaking the molds that have brought us to this point in our journey, we will not have the strength to move forward. Moses left the royal family of Egypt because he wanted to discover who he was and the unique gift he had to offer the world. He could no longer stomach the pain of feeling out of place and the constant restlessness within.

Jesus, as the Apostle Paul describes, emptied himself of everything, even life, showing others that emptiness is a prerequisite to the transformed life. It is the only hope we have to be holy and activate the eternal gift within each and every one of us.

The kingdom of God is not something we are promised in the future. It is now. It involves opening ourselves, our minds, and our hearts to new things. It is the things that we have not heard, the things we have not seen, and have yet to even cross our minds that will draw us forward.

We cannot be transformed if we are full of ourselves. Jesus said that unless a seed dies, it cannot bear fruit. A dying to self, a destruction, is what is required. And the courage to do so will confirm for us that we are living from a life force deep within us.

To live with that posture toward the world will reveal the slender threads that so carefully lead down the path to something better, more secure, and something eternal.

The Magician can only work within us as much as we will allow. So if you are restless as you read this, know it is evidence that the invitation to transformation is already taking place. Open the eyes of your heart, watch closely, and carefully observe where the slender threads will take you next.

Chapter Seven in Review

To Reflect On

- We all have those moments where we secretly wonder if someone or something else is in control of the universe, connecting the dots.

- The magic the Magician releases in our live when we are open to change is through the slender threads that connect one event to the next, one relationship to the next.

- Everyone has had one of those moments where you felt like everything in the universe aligned at the right time.

- No matter where you are today, you were not designed to stay there, unchanged.

- If we reject the uncomfortable and unfamiliar, the Magician will not have permission to work within us to bring us into alignment with our deepest desires.

- Living in an age of distractions, the irony is that we can't connect with anyone or anything until we are grounded in an understanding of who we are.

- The truth is, change affects us before it affects anyone else.

- Change rarely comes to us as profound and epic.

- When we stop asking good questions, we limit—or even prohibit—the change that needs to take place in our lives.

- The connection between the world we see and the world we do not see is much more profound than we might first think.

- It is our curiosity and openness to the possibility that something closer to our true selves exists in front of us that keeps us moving forward.
- No one person, circumstance, or construct is big enough to hold you and captivate you forever.
- We cannot be transformed if we are full of ourselves.
- Feeling restless is evidence that transformation is already taking place.

To Ponder and Discuss

- Describe a time when seemingly disconnected things seemed connected. What happened? What did you learn?
- Why do we say we want change but try to avoid feeling uncomfortable and the unfamiliar?
- Why is change within more important than change without? What happens if we try to change others before we try to change ourselves?
- List the people who have played the role of mentor or guru for you, even if only for a short time. Summarize what you learned from each person.
- How does feeling restless confirm transformation is taking place?

CHAPTER EIGHT

Living Beyond Our Balance Sheets

The choices we make, the curves we are thrown, the chances we take, the hunches we follow are all part of our mysterious journey in the direction of who we were whispered into being to become.

—Robert Benson

Confession: I'm addicted to buying and selling gadgets. And eBay is my drug of choice. It is not unusual for me to buy and sell a variety of electronics throughout the year. And I make a little money—or at the very least break even—on most transactions.

Part of what fuels the habit is that I like to use different devices that interest me. I use them for a while and then sell them and move on to the next thing. Over time, I've learned to buy what will sell. I've also learned what to do to help make products move faster through offering bonuses like free shipping.

This habit drives my wife crazy. She is a buy-one-thing-and-use-it-until-it-dies kind of person. I'm all about new experiences and changing up habits and routines. And I figure that if I can at least break even, then it is not a bad hobby to have.

But what I love more than the gadgets or even the incredibly smooth selling process on eBay is the transaction. I love taking the pictures of item, researching what others are selling the item for, what accessories are available for an item, coming up with a great headline, and writing the copy for the description.

Then I get to decide what price I will list it for, outline the terms of the transaction, preview the listing, and finally let it go live. Most items I list sell within a few days. I anxiously anticipate that wonderful cash register "ching" sound. Along with the notification on my phone comes the knowledge that the item has sold. For a brief moment I feel like I accomplished something.

Yet that feeling of satisfaction is very, very brief. Then I realize I need to find something else to sell. That means I'm going to have to decide which gadget to sell next or find one to buy, use, and then sell soon. It's a never-ending cycle.

What Are You Selling?

To some extent, we all live for some type of transaction. We are all in pursuit of something. And whether you want to admit it or not, everyone is selling something. You might not have that title on your business card, but you have something to sell. It could be an idea, an experience, or whatever. There is no person who is exempt from the transaction process.

Some people like to buy things. Other people like to sell things. Then there are people like me who enjoy both sides of the ledger. If what we want is more important than what it will cost us, we perceive the deal to be advantageous. And on the surface, that logic seems to work.

The flaw in that thinking is that we are in a trap. A transaction only happens for a brief moment, and then it is over. It comes and goes. So in order to replicate the experience of the transaction, we have to look for the next thing.

For many upwardly mobile, achievement-oriented, type-A professionals, the pursuit of what's next is exciting and invigorating. It can captivate your time and attention. And the promise of progress and improvement in income, status, and opportunity can be enough to entice you to exchange things like time, skills, and energy.

The payoff is typically good. It most likely will come in the form of a job promotion, more money, more power (and responsibility), and additional benefits and perks. That transaction works great as long as your assumptions hold true.

Temporary Is Stability

The trouble with the human constructs in which we place our trust and to which we give our lives is that they will pass away. A surgeon can't perform his or her duties without hands. A truck driver can't drive if he or she goes blind. And a musician is unlikely to continue to perform at his or her peak potential if he or she can no longer hear.

The word that resonates with me as I think about those frightful years of 2000 to 2010 is *temporary*. What we hold onto now is temporary. What we cling to for meaning, hope, and inspiration is all temporary.

Our kids will grow up. Our job will eventually no longer be necessary. The things we do today were likely not even in existence ten years ago. And what we will be doing in ten years has yet to be invented. This is the world we live in.

Transformation is temporary, just like everything else in life. The Magician knows this. The things that last are the knowledge that everything is changing all the time. What that means is that while we move through the transformation process, we become keenly aware that our transformation is not for our benefit alone but for the benefit of the community in which we live. It means that we respect people, look for meaningful experiences, and invest in ourselves and others.

Few people will be known for the balances sheets they kept in life. Your legacy will be preserved in the stories people tell about you, the lasting story of transformation that God inspires in you. That is the only thing that remains.

Weathered by Time

I had the opportunity to compete at the national level in student congress in high school. It was hosted at Harvard University that particular year. It was my first trip to Boston.

Even though it was February, I was confident my little wind-breaker would hold up against the cold and chilly weather of the Northeast. When I walked off the plane, I was nearly sliced in two by the wind that passed over me. I had never been so cold in my life.

One of the things I wanted to do while I was in Boston was walk the Freedom Trail. Never mind that a blizzard was going on outside. I was young and stupid, so naturally I thought, *How cold could it really be?*

I nearly froze to death. As often as I could, I stopped and went into a little shop or restaurant, even if only for few minutes, to warm up and then get the courage to start down the pathway again. It seemed to take forever. But I wanted to walk that path more than I wanted to be warm.

I remember coming to a very old graveyard where some famous people were buried. As I walked through the rows of tombstones, I noticed that some were so worn you couldn't even read the name or dates anymore. It was as if they had been erased from this world.

No one knew what type of buggy they owned, how much land they possessed, the success of their business, or the amount of money they accumulated. And without some type of notes or official records, I didn't even know enough about them to Google them to see if I could find out more. The only hope they had of not being for-gotten at this point was to be contained in the stories that the people they loved told about them.

In the Gospels, Jesus questioned the benefit of exchanging our souls for the empty promises of the things that are temporary. How sad a commentary it would be to have spent our whole lives transacting every part of our lives only to realize that we failed to read the fine print.

If Jesus was onto something, it was this: everything is temporary. Our lives, time, money, relationships, responsibilities, and so on. Everything. Not one thing we own, possess, or work for will last forever. Life is a state of being in constant motion. The question becomes, *what are we moving toward?*

Even the process of being transformed is temporary. It doesn't last forever. It may repeat itself in our lives, but the role of the Magician only takes us to the point at which we are ready to give in to our deepest fears, give up our grip on the things we perceive to be eternal, and open up to what we have yet to know, discover, and experience.

What the Magician knows is that when the process of transformation is complete, you will find a sense of freedom, adventure, and passion like you have never known before. It is by breaking the rules that you will discover a different set of rules that govern the substance of life. And those rules are grounded in the principle that what is certain is changing, and what is changing is certain.

The Mystic Within

The most important phase in the process of being transformed has yet to come. You are almost there but not quite ready. There is one thing that is left to put into motion. Before the work of the

Magician is complete within your life, you must agree that another dimension of life exists, one that is beyond time and space.

I'm a hopeless mystic. From an early age, I prayed that I would be able to see other realms of existence that were beyond this physical world. I'm not talking about ghosts and goblins, I'm talking about recognizing that which holds the world together. There is a guiding force within our lives that is much more powerful than we ever imagined, and it's not contained within banks and political powers.

This sense of otherness is important because it becomes the access point we need to see life in a different way. We all find this access point through a variety of paths. But what we are truly seeking is an escape hatch from the insanity that will one day be gone for good.

The power of transformation is not in the hope of what will happen, though that is incredibly important. The power lies in our ability to reach beyond what we know is possible and create change in our lives today. The Magician can take us through the process of change, but if we do not believe, then we can't see. And if we can't see with the eyes of our hearts, then we will always fall short of what we hoped this life would be about.

The magic of change we experience during this phase is only magical if we allow it to be. The steps of transformation go something like this: We can choose to let go of what is holding us captive. We can decide that balance sheets and business cards are not big enough, wide enough, or deep enough to contain the people we were destined to be the moment the Creator breathed new life into us.

And then you must reach forward, leaping from the illusions of certainty that you are most likely becoming much less certain of as you move forward and things become more in focus. It is then that you are at the point of seeing life as more than a temporary transaction. It is the very thing that we think that will kill us that will, in fact, save us.

Holding On by Letting Go

In the biblical story, Abraham was asked by God to sacrifice the son he and his wife, Sarah, had been given well beyond their youth. Abraham did as God had asked. He prepared Isaac as the sacrifice. You can feel the weight of every step Abraham took as he envisioned going to Sarah to say her only child had been made a sacrifice to God. The whole thing just had to feel like a terrible misunderstanding.

So when Abraham raised his instrument of death in the air, with Isaac fully aware of what was about to happen, God stopped him. The man who was promised to be the father of many nations had to willingly let go of the very link (Isaac) to the fulfillment of God's promise before he could become the figure we know as Father Abraham. It was in that moment that Abraham lived into the promise God had made him.

Until we are ready to see beyond what we are sure of, we will never discover the fulfillment of the promise that has been made to us. It is only when we are ready to look beyond the obvious and reject the stable constructs of this human world that we will discover and live into the life force and promise of abundance and satisfaction made to us at the moment of our creation.

But when we do choose to believe, the work of the Magician will be complete. Our transformation will have been accomplished. And we will then be ready to begin the journey back to our community so we can offer ourselves as a gift to others.

The final phase of our journey is, indeed, the most profound. The best is yet to come. Don't be too quick to substitute a temporary transaction for one that will yield a return so valuable not even a balance sheet could measure the shift that will take place in your life.

Chapter Eight in Review

To Reflect On

- We are all in pursuit of something.
- The trouble with the human constructs in which we place our trust and to which we give our lives is that they will pass away.
- What we hold onto now is temporary. What we cling to for meaning, hope, and inspiration is all temporary.
- We will pay to play in this life. And the sum total of our return will be determined by the investments we make.
- The things that last are the knowledge that everything is changing all the time.
- Our transformation is not for our benefit alone but for the benefit of the community in which we live.
- Life is a state of being in constant motion. The question becomes what are we moving toward.
- There is no amount of success, money, or power in this world that can insulate you from change.
- It is by breaking the rules that you will discover a set of rules that govern the substance of life. And those rules are grounded in the principle that what is certain is changing, and what is changing is certain.
- Balance sheets and business cards are not big enough, wide enough, or deep enough to contain the person you were destined to be the moment the Creator breathed new life into you.

- When we are ready to look beyond the obvious and reject the stable constructs of this human world, we will discover and live into the life force and promise of abundance and satisfaction made to us at the moment of our creation.

To Ponder and Discuss

- What transactions are you making in your life today? Are they worth your time and energy?
- What did you learn from events such as 9/11 and the Great Recession? How did those experiences shape you?
- Why is believing in transformation necessary to complete the change process?
- How is it possible that stability is found in a state of perpetual change?
- If your name was worn away on your grave marker, who would tell stories about you? What would they say?

PART THREE

The Hero

The greatest opportunity we have is to accept

the adventure that is before us, embrace inevitable

change, and live into that part of us that was

breathed into us at the moment of our creation.

This allows us to possess something of value to

offer to others and leave the world changed forever.

A Hero—absent of his or her return—will fall short

of experiencing what it means to be fully alive.

CHAPTER NINE

The Paradox of Faith

*The way to become human is to learn to recognize the lin-
eaments of God in all of the wonderful modulations of the
face of man.*

—Joseph Campbell

When I tell people I work in my backyard, they aren't quite sure what to say next. Their puzzled looks make me wonder what exactly they are envisioning in their minds. Are they thinking I just sit down on the grass with a laptop or writing pad? Do they see me sitting in a tent? Who knows exactly what they have in mind the first time they hear me say it, but I can guarantee you when I show them pictures they are blown away. It is far from their first impression.

My first year being self-employed came with a corner in the extra room of the house. The only problem was that we bought the house because the bonus room provided a great space for the kids to play. Now their play time was limited because Dad had to work. I tried to reason with them, but even I wasn't a good enough salesman to pull it off.

I would be on a conference call when one of them would scream or make some loud noise. This was not exactly professional, but it was functional, and we made it work as long as we had to.

Eventually, there was no more postponing the move. It was time to find my own space. They needed their play room back, and I needed a place to work with a little more security from the unexpected. But I had no idea where I was going to find office space.

A friend told me about an executive office suite he was leasing space from. Everything was provided in the lease. It was really a great deal. For one monthly rate, I had an office with a door, furniture, fully stocked break room, conference room, office equipment such as copiers and printers, utilities, and a cleaning service.

I don't take long to make decisions most times. I reviewed the contract and quickly returned it. I had fully moved into my office by the end of the following week. It was great! I finally had my own space where I could be as noisy or as silent as I needed to be. I loved it. All was good. (Most importantly, I had an endlessly flowing coffeepot.)

About three months into driving back and forth to my newfound freedom, I started to dislike the short commute I had to make. I didn't like going to an office when I worked for somebody else. Now I was working for myself and forcing myself to drive to an office that I was paying for. This was insanity to me, so I started to consider other options.

I checked if there were executive suite buildings any closer to home; going back to working in the bonus room was not an option. I could have leased traditional office space, but that would have been much more expensive, and I would have been responsible for everything. I passed on that idea.

Even though I had hit a roadblock, I wasn't going to let that stop me from finding a solution. I needed a Plan B and quick. But I had no idea what my next move would be.

The Work House

There is an Amish store close to our house that sells storage buildings and play houses. One of my writing mentors purchased something similar to what I had seen displayed on their property. I remember promising myself if I ever made it out on my own, I would buy one and work out of it. Maybe now was a good time to check into it. It couldn't hurt. What did I have to lose?

One afternoon I decided to stop by the little Amish store and tell them what I had hoped to accomplish. They showed me a book of pictures and talked through various details I might be looking for in an office building. Every building they make is custom, so I could make it fit my expectations exactly. As I flipped through the book, I realized they had a section called cottages. They all looked like little homes. In essence, they were. I realized I had found what I was looking for.

With a building permit in hand from the city, I purchased one of their cottages and coordinated with them to finish it, too. I'm not much of an outdoors guy. My idea of camping is the Embassy Suites.

They insulated the walls and floor, put in drywall and flooring, added a thermostat-controlled HVAC system, four large double-paned windows and two dormer windows on top. I wanted it to feel big and let in a lot of light and match the roof shingles on our house.

We hired an electrician, and we added a brick walkway from our back deck. Our landscape guy added some simple plants, bushes, and rocks around the house. When it was all done, it looked almost like a miniature version of our house.

We must have done a good job making it look like a little house because we got someone in the neighborhood all worked up. Shortly after the work was complete, we received a nice (anonymous) note from someone who reminded us our neighborhood rules only allowed for single-family dwellings. They must have thought someone was moving in with us.

I can understand why. When the Amish work, they work as a family. This particular family came to our home almost daily for two to three weeks straight. Even their three-year-old had a paint brush in her hand.

Perhaps what I was most proud of was that I was able to do all of that and fill it full of furniture for about the cost of one year's lease at the executive suite office building. I though it was a great deal, and I couldn't believe it all came together like it did.

The boys call it The Work House. Brooke sometimes calls is The Great Black Hole because I tend to disappear when I close the door behind me. Every once in a while, one of the boys will come out and color in the office while I'm working. I secretly hope that they are learning there is more than one way to work. I hope it inspires them to think beyond the boundaries and follow their passions—even if it takes them as far away as their backyards.

When it was all said and done, I remember just sitting in my new two-hundred-square-foot office with porch thinking about my journey to this point. It was a profound moment, one of those times when your faith, which at times can seem farfetched, becomes real.

The Creative Within

As I sat on my new couch, I remembered the first time my writing mentor showed me his work house more than ten years ago. I thought it was the coolest thing I'd ever seen. And as much as I wanted it, I never really believed that would ever be my reality.

Shortly after I graduated from college, I had a dream. I was working in a room where I was surrounded by books. I was at a computer typing away at a blank screen. It felt very natural and as if it were something more than just an evening hobby. It felt like I was watching myself doing the work I was meant to do. I had no idea how that dream would play out. I certainly didn't consider it a suggestion of what might be true in my near future.

Ten years after that dream, I am now working in The Work House doing the things I only dreamed were possible. Before anyone believed I could do it, I envisioned it and apparently never let go of the vision. I wish I could say I knew after that dream what would take place next. I didn't. And I gave up many times along the way. But it wasn't long after I gave up that I tried to push toward my dream again.

The Work House represents so much more than just a place to work. It is a mile marker in my life because it is something that came from deep within me. I helped create it and bring it into reality. If you've never had an experience like it, it is one of the most amazing feelings in the world. It made me feel fully alive, which leads me to believe that the Creator left a little creative acumen within each of us at the moment of our creation.

And our job is not simply to be artists, painters, and writers. If everyone were an artist in the traditional sense, there would be nothing to draw, paint, or write about. But just because we don't practice the arts doesn't mean we are not an artist in our own way. It simply requires belief in our ability to bring our deepest longings— and the dreams God gives us—into reality. Another way to say it is this: all we need is faith.

A Genie in a Bottle

Faith is seeing outside the physical world and bringing that vision into reality. Faith without action is just a dream. It only makes sense that the children of the Creator are creators in their own right, too. It takes focus and a lot of hard work, but whatever is in your head can come true if you want it badly enough. More important, it must come true because in doing so you'll discover the unique gift you were given to offer the world.

Sometimes we think faith is like a genie in a bottle. If we rub our dreams in just the right way, then—poof!—the world will be as we want it be. But that can't be true. It denies the process of transformation that is always taking place around us and in us. Faith is not an à la carte promise to grant our shallow wishes. It is the process we lean into as we work out the passion and person we were created to become.

The truth is, God is everywhere. One direction isn't any holier than another. What makes it holy is how we approach it. Are we living with our hands open, waiting to learn, grow, and give back? Or are we sitting with our arms crossed waiting for what is rightfully ours to come to us?

Faith is not simply something that we receive or practice; it is what we give the world. After disruption has taken place and the Magician's work is complete, we are ready to enter back into the community—only we come back not with a grudge but with a gift to offer. And that gift will look different and function differently depending on the person and the circumstances. But the fundamental aspect of the gift we will bring back to others is a knowledge and awareness that faith is what will take us to the desert, and it will be faith that will bring us into the promised land of our lives.

The paradox of faith is we do not comprehend it until we practice it, and we cannot possess it until we give it away. It is something that has been freely given to you and me. So, naturally, it should be freely given away to others.

An Unofficial Chapel

Every month a friend and retired Episcopal priest comes by The Work House for conversation and to celebrate the Eucharist with me. Geoffrey is one of those people who you will meet and never forget. He is quiet and reserved. Yet there is something about him that just draws you in. He passes no judgment and holds no grudges toward anyone. He is the most present, open, and caring minister I've ever known. And for some reason we connected and haven't looked back since.

We first met during the midweek Eucharist services at the cathedral where I put the pieces of my life back together. It was not unusual for us to stay after the Eucharist celebration was over and talk about life, hurts, dreams, and passions. I just enjoyed being in his presence. He is one of those people who makes you feel good about yourself and cheers you on even when you are struggling to make sense of everything.

After I built my Work House, I thought I'd call Geoffrey. I knew he didn't live far from my house. I thought maybe he wouldn't mind coming by every now and again so we could talk and share the Eucharist together. He was delighted and quickly accepted my invitation.

So once every thirty days or so, Geoffrey comes by The Work House for conversation and Communion. For a couple hours every month, all the alerts on my computer are silenced, my phone is turned off, and my office is transformed into a chapel.

Each time he comes over we spend the first hour or so just talking. We share conversation about life. We ask questions of one another. And we celebrate the ups and downs we experience individually. I feel privileged to listen to someone who has listened so closely to his own life and has had the courage to become the person he is today. That doesn't happen by accident but through authentic faith.

When the conversation is over, we know it is time to pray. We push aside anything that is on the coffee table that sits just in front of the sofa and turn it into an altar. He gracefully puts on his stole and opens the portable Communion kit that he's probably used for more than four decades in ministry.

Once the elements are ready, we read through a liturgy he put together. The core of our celebration is grounded in the *Book of Common Prayer*. In that moment, everything seems to come to focus. We read the same words every month. We repeat the same practices. And yet each time we share the Eucharist, it feels new all over again.

Faith makes it possible for old things to become new and new things to become old. Faith gives us the strength to push through times we are weak and accelerates our effort when we are strong. Faith is the confidence we need to continue to push forward even when the outcome is not clear.

Unexpected Heroes

The last and final person we meet on our journey is the Hero. The word *hero* means a lot of things to a lot of different people. There are the Horatio Alger stories of early Americans who pulled themselves up by their own bootstraps. Then there is the John Wayne character, the strong and relatively silent type who acts on his gut and follows his instinct where it leads. But for me, the Hero most likely to change the world looks and acts a lot more like Geoffrey than John Wayne.

The idea of the Hero, at least in the context of our conversation, is not someone who acts alone but someone who acts on behalf of others. A Hero is not someone who operates on behalf of his or her own goodwill. Rather, a Hero is someone who returns from a journey of personal transformation with a unique gift to offer the community that originally forced him or her out.

Like faith, the journey of the Hero will first lead you away, then it will lead you through, and finally, it will lead you back. That's why I vehemently resist the idea that anyone can lose faith. If faith could be lost, then it would be something we could take up and put down based on a whim or our personal volition. Instead, faith will carry us through even the times when we aren't strong enough to acknowledge it.

I can think of no one who has done more exploratory work around the Hero's journey than Joseph Campbell. His books showed us that the Hero is not the one who saves himself or herself but who saves others. The Hero is guided by something deep within that keeps him or her on the move, even through dramatic trials and obstacles. Through every situation, the Hero is shaped and molded into something new. And when it is time, the Hero will return to the community with something unique to offer them, something that will help others, a gift given with generosity of heart and mind.

One way we will know that transformation has taken place in our lives is that our perspectives will change. We'll begin to realize that faith operates at a different cadence than the pace we often set for ourselves. And, in turn, we'll adjust and adapt throughout the seasons of our life to the change that is always happening around us.

As we work to balance the inner world with the outer world, we must find our own Work Houses to provide a safe place where we can work and explore the very gifts we have been given to share. And we must find our own Geoffreys who will remind us that faith is about prayer and prayer is about being changed again and again. The paradox of faith is that it leaves us with a belief in the power of the creative force that lies within, even if we don't recognize it in ourselves at first. It's not ours for the taking, but it is ours for the making.

Chapter Nine in Review

To Reflect On

- The Creator left creative acumen within each of us at the moment of our creation.

- It only makes sense that the children of the Creator are creators in their own right, too.

- Faith is the process we lean into as we work out the passion and person we were created to become.

- The truth is, God is everywhere. One direction isn't any holier than another.

- Faith is not simply something that we receive or practice; it is what we give the world.

- The fundamental aspect of the gift we will bring back to others is a knowledge and awareness that faith is what will take us to the desert, and it will be faith that will bring us into the promised land of our lives.

- The paradox of faith is that we do not comprehend it until we practice it, and we cannot possess it until we give it away.

- Faith is the confidence we need to continue to push forward even when the outcome is not clear.

- A Hero is someone who returns from a journey of personal transformation with a unique gift to offer the community that originally forced him or her out.

- Like faith, the journey of the Hero will first lead you away, then it will lead you through, and finally, it will lead you back.
- One way we will know that transformation has taken place in our lives is that our perspectives will change.
- It's not ours for the taking, but it is ours for the making.

To Ponder and Discuss

- What were you taught about faith as a child?
- Have you ever created something from nothing? Describe what happened. What did that experience teach you?
- Why are there so many definitions of a hero in today's culture? Which one resonates with you?
- Who is someone who has been an anchor for you in your life? What have you learned from this person?
- Why is faith so important to the journey of transformation?

CHAPTER TEN

Doing Is the New Believing

A man is raised up from the earth by two wings—simplicity and purity. There must be simplicity in his intention and purity in his desires. Simplicity leads to God, purity embraces and enjoys him.
—Thomas à Kempis, *The Imitation of Christ*

Sometimes someone says something to you that you never forget. I don't remember the day or time, but I do remember exactly what was said. And my suspicion is that it came in the midst of an everyday conversation over half a grilled cheese sandwich and a bowl of chili at a local restaurant and pub in town.

I first met this particular mentor through a mutual acquaintance. I sent Robert a handwritten note one day and asked if we could meet. I wanted to ask him a few simple questions. I suspect he knew, judging by the effort I expended to reach him (not many people write handwritten notes anymore), that I was serious. And I suspect he also knew that I might have undersold just how simple the questions were. Nonetheless, he agreed to meet.

The irony of it all was that we spent most of our first meeting on a bench on Church Street. Since we both find a lot of meaning in the sights, sounds, and practice of the Christian tradition as contained within the monastic and traditional liturgies, the mere suggestion of meeting on Church Street was fitting. We talked about a number of things that day, which ultimately led to a friendship that continues to this day.

We agreed to meet every month or so. We set the rules: always be honest, and take turns paying for lunch. This seemed like a fair trade. Our conversations varied from lunch to lunch, but there was something deep within me that confirmed this person had something compelling: a wisdom that typically emerged in a totally unexpected moment of our conversation.

We all should have someone in our lives who cheers us on as we move through life. And it probably needs to be someone separate from our spouse. It needs to be someone who has nothing to lose if they make us upset or frustrated. It needs to be someone who is a few steps removed from our lives so they can speak without concern that one of us is going to end up sleeping on the couch that night.

I'm not suggesting that your spouse can't speak into your life. Your spouse should. Yet no matter how clear I feel I am on things, certain people in my life—including my spouse—seem to have better perspective than I do. So I listen.

So when my mentor said these four sentences, it stopped me dead in my tracks. We were talking about the usual things: writing, making your life count, struggling to make sense of the urgings that I felt and the pressure to fall in line with the permission systems that the world had set for me as a professional. He said, "Everyone gets twenty-four hours a day, no matter how much you try to squeeze in it or out of it. And those twenty-four hours come in sixty-minute increments. You can't speed it up. You can't slow it down. It's what you do with it that matters."

That probably seems obvious to you. But for someone who tries to overachieve in absolutely every area of his life, it hit me like a ton of bricks. No matter how hard I work, no matter how hard I try, no matter how hard I want something to be true, I don't have any more or less opportunity than the next person. I am ordinary. We all are ordinary. And the opportunity to do something extraordinary is available to anyone who wishes to make it so.

This Ordinary Life

What makes life ordinary is not that we have the same opportunities, begin in the same way, or even are given all the same chances in life. That would be boring and would only manufacture people rather than let them live into their own personal uniqueness. What makes life ordinary is that everyone must decide the type of life he or she is going to live. It is not something that is thrust upon us but something that is ours for the taking.

There will absolutely be things happen in your life that you didn't expect. That's part of what makes you different from me. But that doesn't change the amount of time we have or the pace in which we experience that time. The clock runs the same whether you are looking at it or I am. In spite of what those TV infomercials might suggest, there is no way to turn back time. You are the sum total of what you choose to do with the time you have been given.

That means in order for us to live into being the people we were created to be at the moment of our creation, we must act on what we know to be true, right, and pure. Purity is not perfection. Purity is alignment between our deepest longing and that which brings us our greatest satisfaction.

We get to create our lives at a pace that is predictable. There may be moments when time seems to stand still. Or there may be moments when we are so caught up in the experience that time seems to fade into the background and disappear. But the clock is still ticking. And if we hope to experience the fullness of life, we must choose to start living today.

Watercolor Pictures

One of my favorite Bible stories as a child was Peter walking on the water. I can still see the watercolor picture in my children's

Bible that depicted the scene. I remember wondering what it must have been like for Peter the moment Jesus saves him from drowning; I imagined that in that one experience Peter knew his destiny and never went off course again. He moved forward for the rest of his life without question or hesitation.

Only that's not exactly how it happened. My suspicion is that Peter got out of the boat because he was mad at Jesus. He also didn't want to back down from a challenge in front of his best friends. He had a reputation to uphold. If he were to fail to accept Jesus' invitation, he would have a lot of explaining to do. And Peter was someone who'd rather fail at trying than fail to try.

So he got out of the boat. The adrenaline was likely rushing through his body. It took him a few minutes to realize he wasn't in a safe place anymore. And when he did, he panicked. All he could think about was getting back in the boat. Finally, Jesus comes right to him and lifts him out of the water and helps him back into the boat.

I like Peter. He is brash at times. He isn't scared of a good fight. He lives with a reasonable amount of skepticism about everyone and everything. Peter also isn't afraid of a good challenge. Even better is the surprise that the very guy who denied Jesus is the guy who would later be described as the rock on which the church would be established.

How's that for a turn of events? If you think that denying God's will is a sure way to lose your faith, think again. It may be that in that denial, we discover what we really believe in the first place.

My Life Philosophy

I have a philosophy in life: doing is the new believing. I'm all about pomp and circumstance. But if changing ourselves and changing the world around us is important, then we must exert some type of force upon the world. In order to offer something unique that benefits others, we must be ready to take action.

Peter jumped out of the boat before he had fully accounted for his surroundings. He sliced off the ear of the Roman solider before Jesus had a chance to surrender and be taken into custody. Peter denied Jesus three times before he had to a chance to explain he was scared and frustrated.

That same person would later preach what is arguably the most successful sermon in all church history. He was true to his Jewish roots but realized that the separation between Jews and non-Jews might have been a big deal for his contemporaries but was incompatible with the person of Jesus and the freedom he preached.

Peter didn't work out his faith in the back pew of a cathedral. Peter worked out his faith in the midst of the people he wanted to tell about this Jesus who changed everything. He took the passion and energy within him and put it into motion.

Yes, he had to course correct at times. Yes, he changed his mind as he matured in his faith. And yes, he fumbled the ball regularly. But he fumbled the ball heading down the field. He was on the turf. And moving.

This is what my mentor was trying to tell me. The opportunities will come. The time to break out will come. The moments to discover what is really, truly inside will come. And you will eventually discover the unique gift you have to offer others.

Our job is not to plan, orchestrate, or manipulate our way into those experiences. Our job is to show up, lean into the moment, and allow it to take our breath away. This is what it means to be fully alive, fully present, and ready to embrace the chaos and uncertainty of the world around us.

A Gift to Offer

The Power of Half is a book about a family that many aspire to be a part of: two parents and two children. One boy and one girl. Dad works hard and makes it big in his field. Mom is the glue who holds the family together. They are, by many social standards, the perfect family.

This family lived a dream life. They owned a very large home. They drove big SUVs. And every member of the family possessed just about everything one might think they need to be happy and content.

Then one day the sixteen-year-old daughter encountered a homeless man. She was disturbed. It's not that the homeless person assaulted her or caused her harm in any way. She was disturbed because something within her was awakened. And it was a restlessness that she couldn't ignore.

So she talked to her family about what she was thinking and feeling. Over time, they began to share her concern. The last one to open up to the idea of helping homeless people out in some meaningful way was her brother. But even he eventually understood the potential to make a significant difference.

The family realized that their efforts to strive for the ultimate experience of the American dream has left them with a great deal of comfort yet plenty of distraction from real life and each other. Perhaps the daughter was onto something. Eventually, they decided to do something about it.

This family didn't just open their checkbook and write a big check, which they could have easily done. That would have been very helpful indeed to some charity who shared their newfound passion for homeless people. They could have hosted a charity event for their closest friends and likely raised a significant amount of money to support homelessness in their city. But that didn't seem disruptive enough for this family.

Instead, they decided to sell their mansion of a house, move into a house half as big, and give away half the proceeds to charity. That amount totaled approximately $800,000. They were so taken by the passion of their daughter that they began to believe in their ability to make a real difference in the world.

Get Dirty!

We can choose to pay our respects to life and hope for the best and expect that to be enough to satisfy our souls. Or we can roll up our sleeves, let go of the comfortable things, people, and circumstances that we are holding onto, and look for ways to get involved.

There is no way a Hero can return to the community and fulfill his or her journey unless he or she gets personally involved in some way. That means the opportunity for risk is high, and so is the possibility of failure.

You might go bankrupt. You might feel regret. You might make a bad decision. You might turn in the wrong direction. You might disregard good advice and follow bad advice.

But just as your mind can race toward what bad things might happen, you could make room for good things to happen, too. You could discover a new way to live. You could find happiness in places you didn't expect. And you could uncover a path that you didn't even see was right in front of you.

None of that happens if you just sit in the boat and wait for the safety of the shore to find you. In fact, you'll starve your soul and die inside out if you do. The illusions that you've worked so hard to let go of will continue to haunt you. Some of them may never go away. That's why the Outlaw and the Magician will come again in your life.

But for now you are called to finish the journey that is ahead for you, putting one foot in front of the other. When you do, you'll discover you are so close to discovering who you were breathed into existence to be—and yet you might still not recognize it.

People look at the life I lead from the outside in. They see the passion I have for the work I do. They sense the adventure. And they wonder how they can have it, too. But I'm making my life up as I go along, I explain to them. I have thrown away the map. I've rejected the illusions that someone else will provide any sense of safety, stability, and security. And I've refused to follow any path that doesn't light me up inside.

Scared to Death

The truth is I live most of the time scared to death of all the things that could go wrong, but I keep moving forward. There is something that swells deep within me every time I want to quit and give up. It keeps pulling me toward something that I have yet to fully realize and may not this side of eternity.

The scariest obstacles, the darkest places, and the unrelenting doubt are the breeding ground of heroic deeds. They are heroic not because they are beyond the capacity of humanity to accomplish. Rather, they are heroic because you are brave enough to face yourself and the illusions of the limitations you have willingly placed on your life.

The Hero knows you have the ability to break through the voices in your head. The Hero knows you have the ability to rise above whatever impossible odds seem stacked against you. The Hero knows you will make it back alive because you have something only you can give to the world.

The world is not against you. This is a war that is fought within you, not among other people.

This is a battle for your mind, body, and spirit to work in sync with the life force deep within you. And you only begin to bring all the different elements of yourself together when you start to move forward.

Momentum is what the Hero knows will bring all of you into alignment. And once you are aligned, then you can move forward with reckless abandon, unencumbered by the illusions that have interrupted so many others on their journey.

The End Is a Beginning

The moments when it seems like it is easier to give up than go on, keep pushing. The times when it seems like jumping off is more predictable than staying the course, hold your position. The sense that you are coming to the end is really your true self recognizing a new beginning.

The actions that we take, the decisions that we make, and the things we choose to give ourselves to are the substance of our lives. If we don't like the current mix, we can change it up. This is our life, and it is the only life we were meant to live. It's not our job to live someone else's life. It's not our responsibility or obligation to fulfill someone else's expectations. This is about us, who we were created to be, the moment the Creator breathed life into us.

We can blame everyone else for keeping us from the life we know we were meant to live. It's a cop-out, an easy way to shift blame to someone else. It's a pain-management technique used to avoid the internal struggle we must endure through the Outlaw and the Magician.

The Hero knows that the obligation to offer his or her gift to the community is more important than his or her desire to avoid the pain of searching for, discovering, and refining that gift.

As we put our lives into motion, certainty and confidence will announce the arrival of clarity and conviction. It is in believing that we prepare to act, but it is in doing that we discover what we truly believe. The Creator is not someone who rests but who is actively engaged in the world. The creative remnant within you is begging to be awakened. When you act on your hunches and your intuition, you discover the life you've always dreamed about is more real than you ever imagined.

Chapter Ten in Review

To Reflect On

- No matter how hard we work, no matter how hard we try, no matter how much we want something to be true, we don't have any more or less opportunity than the next person.
- The opportunity to do something extraordinary is available to anyone who wishes to make it so.
- What makes life ordinary is that everyone must decide the type of life he or she is going to live.
- You are the sum total of what you choose to do with the time you have been given.
- Purity is alignment between our deepest longing and that which brings us our greatest satisfaction.
- If we hope to experience the fullness of this life, we must choose to start living today.
- It is in the doing that we discover what we really believe in the first place.
- My job is to show up, lean into the moment, and allow it to take my breath away.
- There is no way a Hero can return to the community and fulfill his or her journey unless he or she gets personally involved in some way.
- The scariest obstacles, the darkest places, and the unrelenting doubt are the breeding ground of heroic deeds.

- Once you are aligned, then you can move forward with reckless abandon, unencumbered by the illusions that have interrupted so many others on their journey.
- The actions that we take, the decisions that we make, and the things we choose to give ourselves to are the substance of our lives.
- You only have one life to live; it might as well be yours and not somebody else's.
- Act on your hunches and your intuition; in doing so you will discover the life you've always dreamed about is more real than you ever imagined.

To Ponder and Discuss

- If you had to describe your philosophy of life in thirty words or less, what would you say?
- Do you believe you have the ability to choose the life you live? Describe an experience where you acted on this belief.
- Why is it easier to be philosopher in the pew rather than a practioner among the people?
- How does alignment between your gift and the needs of the community affect each other? Is your life in alignment? Why or why not?
- What role do actions play in shaping what we believe? Why do we often wait until we believe before we feel comfortable taking action?

CHAPTER ELEVEN

Rediscover the Creator Within

My time I divide as follows: the one half I sleep; the other half I dream.

—Søren Kierkegaard

My oldest son loves Legos. He is fascinated by how the different pieces fit together. He will sit for hours carefully putting the puzzle together piece by piece. I sit for hours worrying about where we are going to put it when he has finished his building project, or how we will keep his little brother (or the cat for that matter) from scattering hundreds of little plastic pieces around the house.

But watching your child discover that he enjoys something and is good at it is an amazing thing. This brings a parent a lot of pleasure.

Not just because your child is captivated (finally) by something for longer than ten minutes, but because he is learning how to see something in his mind and bring that something into reality.

Carter puts together the Lego sets we get for him faster than anyone I've ever seen before. It is not unusual for him to put together a thousand-piece set in about three hours. It's fascinating to watch. He is so serious and so determined. I only wish I could bottle up his determination and take a dose of it from time to time. It has never occurred to him that he can't put a Lego model together. I hope that thought never crosses his mind.

To encourage him, we purchased tubs of different pieces. These, of course, are carefully stowed in an official Lego organization cart that is also color coded. This gives Carter the ability to put together any random pieces and create something without a set of instructions or box to follow. I'm amazed at what his mind will allow him to see and his tenacity to figure out what that looks like in Lego form.

As Carter gets older, his creativity is showing in other areas, too. He is learning to write stories in his first grade class. And these are book-length stories that carry a single idea from beginning to end. If I ever run out of ideas, I may ask him for a few of his.

He'll write these books, draw some illustrations, put it together, and then read it to us. Brooke and I love hearing him read his stories to us! Most important, what he writes make sense, and his characters seem real.

But my favorite part of Carter's creativity is that he keeps a Moleskine notebook of ideas of various things he'd like to invent one day. When he thinks of something, it goes in the notebook along with a picture. Carter can tell you what prompted the idea and how it solves the problem at hand.

At seven years old, Carter is already discovering unlimited ways he can use what he knows and his experience to create something that would solve a particular problem. And he's often sharing that with his little brother.

Something New

The older we get the more likely it is that we'll stop paying attention to our own ideas about how we could improve the world around us. We buy into the lie that following the leader is the best strategy, without being concerned where the leader is going most of the time. If the Hero's work is to be complete, he or she must come back to the community with something new to offer.

This is not new in the sense that no one has ever thought about it before, but new in the sense that the way you see it and the way you go about doing it are different and unique from other people. There are an infinite number of ways to be a manager, CEO, engineer, lawyer, and accountant. You don't have to be a musician, record executive, writer, or publisher to be creative. You don't have to work at an advertising agency or even have *creative* in your job title.

What makes you creative is that you possess something unique within you that all can benefit from. The key is digging deep enough to discover it and, when you do, finding the courage to bring it out of yourself so that others can benefit from it, too.

But somewhere along the way that breaks down. We become more cynical. We stop being encouraged to try new things. We are saddled with responsibility, which means the stakes are higher, the risk appears more ominous, and the payout appears much less likely. So we give up and give in to the rules set for us by others.

When we give up and give in, we convince ourselves that it doesn't matter. Someone else will think of it. Someone else will do it. For a period of time we might be able to ignore it. But it will eventually rise to the top. We can't prevent it. The only appropriate response is to say yes—to the opportunity and to the adventure.

Surrender to Yourself

The most important step in this final phase of your Hero journey is surrender. It is giving up on the idea that someone else knows better. No one can see through the eyes of your heart. No one else knows what you've experienced and how that has uniquely prepared or shaped you for what is in front of you.

You are the only *you* in the entire universe. If you are not you, then there will never be another you. It would be a shame to go through life and never appreciate, respect, and celebrate yourself.

Like many children, my parents enrolled me in piano lessons. I was OK with it because I loved music. It carried me to places I didn't know existed. My favorite music generally didn't have words, and if it did, they were in a language I didn't understand.

There would usually be an hour or so between my getting home from school and one of my parents getting home. As soon as I got home, I either called my dad at work or he called me at a particular time. We had a signal. If the phone rang once, stopped, and then rang twice, it was him. It was safe to answer. He would ask me about my day, make sure everything was OK at the house, and then tell me he'd see me soon.

After I hung up the phone, it was time to get creative. I would sit down at our piano and play. I usually started with some sheet music and practiced what I needed for my upcoming lesson. Then I shut my books and just started playing. I doubt much of it makes sense to the human ear, but it was magical for me. When I played, it was as if the entire world were suspended in time. I felt as if I touched a very deep place within myself.

I played for as along as I could. As soon as I heard the garage door open, my eternity would end. I would come back to reality. I would close the piano key cover, slide the bench back in, and move onto something else.

My parents were always affirming and interested in what I was interested in. There was no reason for me not to let them hear me play. But I was slightly embarrassed to do so. I was so vulnerable in that moment that I didn't want them to see me so exposed, which is a strange thing to feel about the two people who had seen me as exposed as anyone might.

Later in the evening, I would place headphones on while I studied and listen to more music. It would allow me to concentrate and shut down the random thoughts that seemed to constantly be running through my head. The music helped me focus on what I was doing.

For me, music was an escape from all the limitations and boundaries in the world. There weren't any rules to follow. Sure, there were notes on the page and a certain beat to follow. There was a cadence to every song, yet it seemed to disappear.

Exposed and Vulnerable

Creativity is hard not because we do not have the capacity to offer it to others. It is hard because is requires us to let down our guard and expose our deepest experiences to the world. It is hard because we worry we might run out of it at some point in the near future. We worry that people won't like what they see or hear. We worry what bad things might happen if it offends someone or makes them uncomfortable.

All of our hesitations and inhibitions come directly from the permissions systems of a culture that have been predefined and thrust upon us. And we are supposed to accept those as truth and without question. Even worse, we are expected to defend them when those permission systems are called in question or even threatened.

As we get older, we tend to become more willing to exchange creativity for confidence that we'll fit in if we just follow the rules. And somewhere along the way we lose our souls in the process, too. We stop asking ourselves important questions, and we stop expecting an answer that can't be found in any infinite number of step-by-step books that clutters the isles of bookstores and libraries.

But all is not lost. For anyone who has had the courage to embrace the Outlaw and disrupt, confront, and remove the barriers to change, you have discovered your own strength. If you have had the curiosity to subject yourself to the work of the Magician who changed you within, you have discovered that any limitation is a mere illusion and doesn't really exist. Now you must take that last step and act on what you know to be true about yourself and the world around you.

Explore Your World

The Hero stumbles into his or her unique gift through creativity and exploration. When we see clearly and our hearts are open, we will learn and discover things about ourselves and the world around us that we didn't know to be true. I learned this when I discovered I was going to be a writer.

In chapter 1, I talked about writing a newspaper column in college—this was something I did, initially, to help fill the void left by drama in my local church. But it did more than fill a void; it was the beginning of discovering my vocation. It was my junior year of college, and there were some significant changes taking place on campus. One administration was leaving, and a new one had come. Their leadership styles were entirely different: one was built around consensus and the other built around authority.

The tension in the atmosphere could be felt across campus, so much so that it seemed very disruptive to the direction of the university itself. I'm sure most people didn't recognize anything had changed, but I tend to pick up on things that aren't necessarily that obvious.

I decided to write an editorial piece and submit it to the editor of the school paper. He loved it and ran it in the next edition of the campus newspaper. To my surprise, it was widely read and commented on across campus. The editor asked me to write a follow up. I obliged his request, having been secretly hoping he would have asked all along.

I wrote the editorials because I felt compelled to express what I was feeling inside. Those two editorials landed me an opportunity to join the writing staff of the campus newspaper my senior year. I knew it was the last time I would be able to rage against the machine without being sued or fired. And I took every opportunity to do so.

As each edition came out, my readership grew. I could hear people talking as I walked across campus, and I overheard professors saying they looked forward to seeing what I would write next.

There must have been something that resonated within a few people because I started to get inside information about decisions being made. I, of course, would write about this things because I felt responsible to the faculty, staff, and students who were largely unaware of these proposed changes. Eventually, people outside the university started cheering me on, too. The administration didn't quite know what to do with me.

Sometime around the midpoint of my senior year, one official from the president's office reached out to me. He took me to lunch and tried his best to make me feel like I was being listened to. I was studying social movement theory at the time, so I was fully aware of what was happening. Later I would be appointed to a board that never met.

Finally, the new president e-mailed me directly. He said he wanted to know what I would have done differently if I were him. I suppose he thought he had stumped me. I wrote back a four-page e-mail with specifics details and course corrections. I doubt he was expecting any response from me, and surely not that response.

The truth is the same experience can awaken more than one mythic archetype within us. For me, this moment represented both the Outlaw—the breaking away—and the Hero—the giving back. While the written word was the vehicle that took me away from the community, it also brought me back into the community.

This demonstrates the reality that as we change, so does our perspective. This explains why we can tell the same story again and again and yet remember details in new ways or find new meaning again and again. Some say our failure is a hint at our future success. Others say it is our suffering that will reveal our salvation. Life and faith are, indeed, a mystery.

Inspired to Create Change

It was during this time I learned I could write something that people wanted to read and that inspired change. I was hooked. I knew I had activated something within me that was big enough to contain my curiosity about life and a variety of subjects as well as my desire to articulate an idea that moved people to do something specific and that could also be measured. Out of that I started to do some freelance writing, but it certainly wasn't enough to make a full-time gig out of it.

I had no idea what to do with that desire after college. No one was hiring a professional disruptor. I didn't have the right degree for a journalist, so no newspaper would look at me. I didn't have the right pedigree for corporate communications, so I didn't get an interview.

I tried to let that part of me die because it was just too difficult to hold onto and too hard to carry within me. Yet in every position I held for nearly a decade before leaping out on my own, I found a way to write about it or to make writing part of my everyday responsibilities.

I was told that I would need to do something significant before I would have the platform to write about it. I was told that I needed to continue in school and gain credentials such as a terminal graduate degree to earn the right to be listened to. But none of the paths that I was told to follow seemed to fit. And neither did any of the positions that I held.

I was successful in everything I did. I outperformed the other people I worked with. I closed deals no one thought was possible. I achieved things that few people expected me to be able to do. Yet no success and no amount of money captured my mind and attention like writing did.

When I write, I find another dimension of reality. Time stops. I forget to eat. It is a place where I feel the most connected with the things that last forever. And there was nothing I could do professionally that made me feel the same way. The same place that I entered when I played the piano before my parents got home as a child was the same place I walked into when I started writing regularly.

So I kept writing. I kept growing my freelance business. Eventually I started writing books for other people. I learned I had a knack for getting inside someone's head and learning to see the world through his or her eyes. I was also enough of an academic that I could separate myself from my point of view and assume someone else's.

And because of this, other people gave me a great excuse to learn how to write books, speeches, newsletters, and so on. I gained experience by vicariously seeing the world through the eyes of people making a significant difference in the world. I wasn't writing my own ideas, but I was just happy that this type of work was growing and occupying even more of my time.

It was difficult because I was already working full time at a job where I traveled and had a good deal of responsibility. I didn't sleep much. In fact, I even fell asleep while driving with Carter (very young at the time) in his car seat one afternoon. We were both OK, but I did wreck the car.

Thankfully, we drifted right onto the curb and not left into oncoming traffic. That was not one of my finer moments as a parent. It was a wake-up call. If I was determined to make something work to the point of pushing my body to the point of exhaustion, then perhaps I needed to pay attention to what was pushing me to do that and adjust as needed.

Align Fear with Opportunity

All of our lives require adjustment. Just as the tires on our car get out of alignment from time to time, we get out of alignment. We forget to pay attention to the signals within because we are too distracted by the expectations of others. We forget what it feels like to exist in a moment where time stops and we are the best expression of ourselves.

So we do what most people do and settle. We come to grips with the reality that our lives may be as good as they are going to get. But we can't allow ourselves to fall into this temptation because it denies the very remnants of the Creator that exist within each of us.

The challenge the Hero presents to us is not just to take action and move forward but to move in a direction where our creativity can bring about an evolution of perspective, knowledge, and enlightenment that will change us—and change others. It is the foolish ones of the world who end up changing it. The rest just get tied up in fighting each other for power and control.

There is no guarantee that our pursuit of the Creator within will be nice, clean, predictable, and tidy. In fact, creativity has nothing to do with what is known. If it is already known, then it has already been created.

That means what you are reaching for in the midst of your restlessness will not be known, understood, or quantified by others. It will most likely be misunderstood, discouraged, and even vilified by those who have yet to begin their own journey of transformation.

But that's what makes the Hero a hero. It is the courage to face your own fears. And when you do, you discover the strength within yourself to endure the discouragement of others until you discover you have something special only you have the power to create and bring to life.

Chapter Eleven in Review

To Reflect On

- The older we get the more likely it is that we'll stop paying attention to our own ideas about how we could improve the world around us.
- What makes you creative is that you possess something unique within yourself that we can benefit from.
- The only appropriate response is to say yes—to the opportunity and to the adventure.
- The most important step in this final phase of your journey is surrender.
- All of our hesitations and inhibitions come directly from the permissions systems of a culture that have been predefined and thrust upon us.
- The only way the Hero stumbles into his or her unique gift is through creativity and exploration.
- All of our lives require adjustment.
- We forget to pay attention to the signals within because we are too distracted by the expectations of others.
- The challenge the Hero presents to us is not just to take action and move forward but to move in a direction where our creativity can bring about an evolution of perspective, knowledge, and enlightenment that will change us—and change others.

- We can't allow ourselves to fall into the temptation to settle because it denies the very remnants of the Creator that exist within each of us.

To Ponder and Discuss

- Think about something creative you did as a child. What did you do? How did other people react to you? How did it make you feel?
- Why are we more likely to settle for what is rather than use our creativity to bring to life what could be?
- What parts of yourself have you given up on? Why?
- If you could do anything or be anyone but yourself right now, who would you be and what would you do? Why can't you be that person and do those things now?
- What are the signs that you are distracted by the expectations of others rather than focused on using your creativity to bring something new into existence? Do you recognize those signs within yourself? Are you ready to make a change?

CHAPTER TWELVE

A Personal Offering

The personality of every man and woman is sacred.

—William Temple

Y ou have something special and unique to offer the world. Even if you aren't sure what it is yet, you do. And this book is an invitation to you to complete the final phase on your journey. You can't stop now. You've come too far. The only step remaining is to rejoin the community that you left and offer the gift you have discovered within yourself to others.

Offering means a lot of things. If you were raised in a traditional church setting, the offering was a plate that was passed across the pews on Sundays. It was a moment when you gave money to support the work of the local church. That is certainly one expression of any offering. But money falls short of the full meaning of what the word means.

When we offer something, we give it away. We do so willingly and freely, without obligation or coercion. If it not something that we choose to do, then it is not an offering. The goal of our offering is likely contributing our time, money, skills, or whatever to achieve a particular goal. It is our part, if you will, in the grand design of what captivates our imagination. When someone shows us a way to achieve that which is most important to us, then we are willing to offer a part—or all—of what we have in order to bring that possibility into reality.

Maybe you have never considered yourself an offering, but you are. Maybe you do not think what you have within you is worth sharing, but it is. And you may never believe you can change your world, but you can.

Whatever is holding you back is merely an illusion. Resist the temptation to believe that illusions are more than what they are. They do not represent actual barriers but are usually our own projections of what we *believe* holds us back. Pushing past our illusions, we come to face to face with the reality that the only obstacle we must overcome is ourselves and our own capacity to limit the personal offering we have to give the world.

It might be uncomfortable to think that what you have to offer is unique and special and has potential to impact your life, community, and world, but do the uncomfortable work to own that. The greatest tragedy in life is to pass through your time on this planet and never understand how your life did or could have impacted someone else's.

Words Matter

No matter where you came from, what neighborhood you live in, what level of education you have achieved, or what job you have, you are more than the labels society and culture put on you. The Creator breathed something unique and special in you at the moment of your creation. And you have an obligation to discover what that is and use it to benefit others. Your responsibility is not to control it, manipulate it, or abuse it. Your job is to release it and watch it multiply through the lives of the people around you.

The people who change the world are not the ones who have the biggest budgets, the most education, or even the most significant opportunities. The people who change the world are largely nameless except to the people whose lives they have changed. They are world changers because they said yes to the needs around them and used what they had within them to the benefit of the people in need.

If we can let go of the need to change the world and begin to see the power in how we can change our lives, the lives of the people we live with, the families we are part of, the people we work with, and others who are in our spheres of influence, then we will see change on a small scale that has ramifications on a large scale. The great conspiracy in the Creator's design is that what is meant to deter us will bring us focus, and what is meant to disrupt our lives will bring about total transformation.

Someone once taught me you don't have to start an international charity to make a difference in the world. You start with shaking someone's hand, looking someone in the eye when he or she talks to you, and maybe even giving someone a hug. It is the small gestures in life that often make the biggest impact.

A particular person had a difficult time in high school. He didn't perceive himself as someone with anything of value to offer the world. At one point, he was even considering taking his own life until a school teacher noticed something wasn't right. She pulled him aside one afternoon, looked him in the eyes, and told him she believed he could anything he wanted to do in life and that he mattered. That small—seemingly inconsequential—conversation changed his life forever.

This individual would later go on to great success in business and even greater success in helping nonprofit leaders learn to use business principles to create more impact. The small offering of a school teacher has saved families from poverty, reinvigorated tired leaders, and raise hundreds of millions of dollars to help make a difference in a variety of ways.

If you don't believe you have something to offer the world, you are mistaken. Perhaps you need to lean harder into the Outlaw and wipe away the layers keeping you from entering the transformation process. Or perhaps you need to open yourself up further to the Magician, who is waiting for you to give up your fight to hang onto the illusions that are passing away and reach for what's next. Because when both phases are complete, you will be ready to see yourself as you are and discover the gift you have to offer the world.

Be You

My youngest son is more sure of himself than I'll ever be. His smile is captivating, and his laugh is contagious. He is simply one of those children who commands attention when he enters a room. He might just take over the world one day in one way or another.

I love joking with him about being other things. I'll ask him, "Are you a dog?" He'll say, "No." I'll ask him, "Are you a frog?" He laughs and says, "No." I'll ask a third time, "Are you a bird?" He'll shake his head and laugh, "No."

"So if you're not any of those things, what are you?" I'll ask. Without missing a beat, he will respond, "I am Caden."

We have this banter regularly. I love to hear him laugh and watch his reaction escalate as I progress through the questions. More important, I love to listen to him declare that he is who he is—and no one or nothing else. I only wish I could be as sure of myself at thirty-three as he is at three.

You have a gift within you. It is your job to do the work necessary to cultivate that gift so that it will be ready to use at the right moment in time.

Look Through, Not Around

I had a dream once, but it wasn't at night while I was sleeping. I was at a high school band competition. I don't remember exactly where I was. I just remember walking onto the field and being overwhelmed by the size of the stadium, especially looking up from the field. I remember thinking to myself just how overwhelming it must be to look up from that same field when the stadium is packed with screaming fans.

For some reason we weren't in any hurry to get started. So I just stood there and looked around for a moment. In a moment, my mind took me to a different place. It was another stadium that was full of people. Only these people weren't cheering; they were listening closely.

There was someone at the podium who was speaking. I had no idea what he was saying, but it must have been important because so many people were looking on with anticipation about what he would say next.

Soon I saw myself as a transparent figure standing next to this speaker. If you looked through this person, you would see me. Every time he would speak, I would write. Every time he would stop, the pen I had in my hand would stop moving. It was as if there were a connection between his speaking and my writing. They were linked somehow.

I never forgot that image in my mind. I had no idea what it meant. I just knew that it suggested something about me that I wasn't ready to understand or even had enough context to make sense of it. But the more I've moved along my journey through life, the clearer its meaning has become. As I started working with high-capacity leaders and helping them communicate their ideas with words across a variety of mediums, it dawned on me that what I saw in my dream that afternoon was what had actually taken place in my life.

My offering to others is to walk alongside leaders and help them accelerate what they are already doing. But the meaning doesn't stop with words on a page. It is constantly evolving, and it will continue to do so as long as I allow myself to evolve with it. If I just allowed the interpretation to be defined by writing, then I would place limits on its application.

In fact, I recently made another shift in my professional life. My writing evolved through some interesting encounters that expanded my work as a freelance writer into running a content development agency. One of my larger clients was owned by a larger entity. The success I was able to create for my client over three years led to an unexpected opportunity to join forces and become part of the leadership team of their parent company.

It was an almost surreal experience to think that the very thing I wanted to do—write—had somehow opened a door that was literally created just for me. Today, I get to use words, sentences, and paragraphs to help organizations across the globe advance their mission and create change in the world. And the best part is I get to cultivate a team of writers, designers, and change makers, which helps me fulfill the Hero phase of this part of my journey.

But the offering you and I have to give is more than the occupation we hold. It is tied to the person we are becoming and the people in our lives to whom we are giving. My offering as a parent is to walk alongside my boys and help them become men. My offering as a husband is to walk alongside my wife as the best expression of God's creativity and design. My offering to myself is to be courageous enough to take the journey of transformation as often as the opportunity presents itself.

This is what I mean when I talk about a personal offering. I'm guilty of limiting the meaning of so many experiences and dreams in my life and not seeing through them. It is larger than titles, corner offices, and corporate perks. It is larger than religious traditions and cultural standards. Our offering is to help others unlock the greatness of the Creator that is already inside them.

If this is our focus, then we will discover one of the great paradoxes of life: helping others will benefit us in some way. That's not why we do it. Rather, it is the cadence of life set in motion at the beginning of time.

The Abbot Within

One of the reasons I find myself envious of the monastic community is that within it exists an abbot. The abbot—the word comes from the Aramaic for "father"—is the head of a monastery. He guides the monastery, ultimately deciding what the community will do and what each individual monk will do and how the monk will do it. Many abbots are flexible and loving—but if you are to exist within the monastery, you must accept the abbot's role as supreme and his decisions as final. Ultimately, the abbot's role is to represent Jesus Christ on earth.

I think everyone would like to have an abbot, particularly in a time of great confusion or uncertainty. I would probably resist the authority of one if it were absolute, but that is another part of me that has yet to be fully released and transformed. Nevertheless, to have someone else direct my steps when I wasn't sure where to step next would be comforting.

If that is something you desire and don't mind the trappings of the monastic tradition, perhaps you should consider joining a religious order. If giving up all ties to your life as you know it is not a reasonable conclusion, then you must learn to follow the Creator within yourself. The reason we need to endure the process of transformation is not because we are bad and need to be reformed. Instead, the gift already within us simply needs to be unleashed so it can then be given freely to the world around us.

You don't necessarily need an abbot, but you do need to find an anchor. For most people, that will mean looking within and moving beyond the constructs and illusions that litter the dimensions of this world that can be measured and quantified. What you are looking for can only be found within.

Time for a Name Change

The Bible tells a story about Jacob wrestling with an angel. He sees someone he doesn't recognize at night and confronts this person. Jacob recognizes that he must fight this person to protect his family and possessions and save his own life. He wrestles with this person throughout the night until the individual touches his thigh and Jacob releases him. The man with whom he wrestles disappears.

During the struggle, Jacob has a conversation with this man. And he declares that Jacob's name is no longer *Jacob* but *Israel*.

This is a significant moment in Jacob's life and in our understanding of how God interacts with us through moments of great stress and ambiguity. Jacob, after all, was on a journey to escape the wrath of his brother whose birthright he had stolen.

One of the techniques ancient writers would use to capture a moment of personal transformation was to make a name change for the character. Words carry a lot of meaning. It was a very effective storytelling technique that was necessary when storytelling existed solely within oral tradition. It signaled to the listeners that some-thing significant had happened in the character's life. Jacob wasn't the only person in biblical literature to be given a name change: Abram became Abraham, Sarai became Sarah, and Saul became Paul.

I can think of no better description of the process of transforma-tion than the truth contained within this story of the human experi-ence. If we change the characteristics of the story ever so slightly, perhaps we'll recognize ourselves in this story, too. I know I do. Another telling of the story might read like this:

We find ourselves wandering in the darkness and wilds of life as we try to escape the illusions that surround us and appear to limit our potential. Soon we discover an intruder. We feel threatened and fear for our lives, so we confront and fight this intruder. In the midst of the struggle, we discover a new dimension of ourselves. In response, we become a different person as represented by a name change. And we are left with scars that remind us where we have been. It is not a pleasant experience, but it leads to the blessing we've been looking for all along.

However you interpret this story, it is an accurate picture of what can happen when we allow ourselves to engage with the feelings and urging we work so hard to suppress. We suppress them because we are fearful they are too countercultural, too out of the ordinary, or too unconventional to ever bring us anything but pain, grief, and sadness.

Don't let yourself think like that. The gift you have to give the world is in you and is you. The Hero understands the journey is not complete until that gift is known, practiced, and shared within the community. If we all follow the lead of the Hero, we will not rule one another. Rather, we will serve one another and respect one another, recognizing that a remnant of the Creator exists within everyone.

Trust the Process

Life is a process. It has no beginning and no end, really. There are only phases. Whatever phase you're in will not last forever. You can choose to ignore the restlessness within you. You can continue to wait for life to become what it once was. But you would only be marking time.

There is no time limit to the process of transformation. We will only progress as long as we are willing to participate in the process. Until then we are stuck in a moment hoping the illusions that we believe are real and the assumptions that we believe are truth will never change. But we'll eventually give up and give in. The question is not if but when.

It is when you finally let go of the constructs of this world that you realize the style of life is marked by an entirely different set of rules and order. You will uncover significance and meaning in places you originally overlooked. You will be infused with curiosity about yourself, others, and the opportunities that exist ahead of you.

Where you are today, know you will not be there long. Nothing lasts forever except the process by which we are changed. If we can grow comfortable in the midst of transformation, the chaos that surrounds us will become fuel for the journey rather than needless distractions filled with unnecessary preoccupations.

Keep moving forward even if you're not sure where it leads. That which draws you in will lead you to the places you've always wanted to go but never believed were possible. This is your life and your offering to the world. We all need you.

Chapter Twelve in Review

To Reflect On

- You have something special and unique to offer the world.

- Whatever is holding you back is merely an illusion.

- As we push past our illusions, we come to face to face with the reality that the only obstacle we must overcome is ourselves and our own capacity to limit the personal offering we have to give the world.

- The people who change the world are largely nameless except to the people whose lives they have changed.

- The great conspiracy in the Creator's design is that what is meant to kill us will bring us life, what is meant to deter us will bring us focus, and what is meant to disrupt our lives will bring about total transformation.

- It is your job to do the work necessary to cultivate the gift within yourself so it is ready to be used at the right moment in time.

- Our offering is to help others unlock the greatness of the Creator that is already inside them.

- Life is a process. It has no beginning and no end.

- It is when you finally let go of the constructs of this world that you realize the style of life is marked by an entirely different set of rules and order.

- If we can grow comfortable in the midst of transformation, the chaos that surrounds us will become fuel for the journey rather than a needless distraction filled with unnecessary preoccupations.

To Ponder and Discuss

- What does the word *offering* mean to you?
- How does our perception of ourselves impact our ability to see what we have to offer others?
- What offering are you giving to others? How have you seen your offering make a difference in someone's life?
- Who has given you something that has made a difference in your life? Make time this week to send them a note or give them a call and let them know what they mean to you.
- Why is it important to find stability in the process of transformation and change?

Conclusion

Take a deep breath. You've come a long way. So many people, books, relationships, and experiences have come and gone in my life, too. I can still remember the ones that had a deep impact on me. I hope the money, time, and energy you invested in this book have been worth it.

Here's one final challenge: give in to your deepest passion and follow the direction you know is right but seems impossible, scary, and overwhelming. It is the only chance you have to discover the greatness already inside you and live into the beauty placed within you at the moment of your creation.

Pay attention to everything, especially that which you hate the most about the world and others: it's an indication of the change that needs to take place within you. Before you can ever hope to live into the full potential breathed into you at the moment of your creation, you must respond to the journey your restlessness is leading you to take. You must be willing to break away and live through separation, transformation, and your return. This is what resurrection is all about.

The story of the resurrection of Christ is powerful for many reasons; among them, it provides a model of what it means to be betrayed, broken, and dead. Yet through that suffering God brought Jesus back to life. And it is through our suffering that we, too, will be brought back to life. The power we have to experience new life, renewal, and rebirth every day is the life force and energy we need to endure the process of transformation and spiritual formation.

In the *Book of Common Prayer*, we read, "By your Spirit, fashion our lives according to the example of your Son, and grant that we may show the power of your love to all among whom we live."[1]

What a beautiful and accurate picture of what can happen within us. The legacy of faith we must leave behind for those who come after us is our own story of resurrection. Our story is the greatest example of what can happen in the life of someone who is willing to live with open hands, ready to accept life in all its fullness.

No one is promised a life filled only with charm, wealth, and good things. Those things don't last anyway. The only way to find the ever-elusive peace that surpasses all understanding is to spend time exploring, shaping, and mending your soul. The problems with the world have nothing to do with people, circumstances, or situations "out there" but have everything to do with what is going on within you. It is much easier to point your finger, pass judgment, and feel certain about the solution when you project your anxiety, fear, and doubt elsewhere.

The next move is in your hands. You can continue to perpetuate a system that is broken. You can continue to stay the course, believing somehow things will get better. You can hope that ladder you so carefully placed along the wall of cultural promises is as tall and stable as you first thought it to be.

But you have another option. You can choose to destroy what holds your confidence today so you are ready to move forward. You can choose to face the illusions of predictable success with your eyes wide open, recognizing that the things you can count on are disruption, change, and transformation.

Journal Exercise

Instructions: *Find a quiet place to reflect and respond to the steps below. Give yourself an attainable goal of completing one question or item at a pace you can sustain. It may be one a month, a week, or even one a day. Finishing this exercise is not as important as exploring the change you want to see take place in your life and understanding how to move forward with confidence.*

1. If you had the power to change your life right now, what would you change about yourself and your circumstances? List them below.

2. Think of a story from your past and a story from your present that have contributed to your desire to make the changes you listed above. What feelings are attached or associated with those stories?

3. Based on your list, write a phrase or sentence about how each of the things on your list makes you feel about yourself, your life, and others.

4. Who is telling you can't make the changes you've listed above? Who is telling you that you can? Who are you listening to?

5. What role will faith play in your pursuit of personal transformation? Is it necessary?

6. List the things that are keeping you from making the changes you want to take place in your life.

7. Name three people you could talk to about the changes you want to make in your life. Beside each name, describe how that person might be able to help you find the courage or determination to move forward.

8. Assign a date to each of the changes you want to make in your life. Determine what steps you need to take to let go of what is holding you back so you can be ready to reach forward to what's next.

9. Visualize your life after you make the changes listed above. Describe what you see. How do you feel? What are you able to do that you couldn't do before?

10. Think of at least three people you can encourage to make a significant changes in their lives. List ways you can guide them to let go and reach forward.

Acknowledgments

I want to say a special thank you to Lil Copan and the Abingdon team for believing in me and my ideas enough to put it on a bookshelf.

To Kyle and David, thanks for representing my work and being good friends.

To Lawrence and Robert, you cheered me on from as early as I can remember. Your willingness to let me into your worlds and show me what it means to live into your passion and giftedness inspired me. I only hope to have the courage you both have to spend a lifetime showing up and doing the work, never knowing exactly where it will lead.

To Ben, Dane, and Geoffrey, your constant push toward that which I have not yet seen has opened me to new things. I only hope to be as holy as the three of you are one day.

To my family, thanks for your love, encouragement, and occasional prodding along the way.

And to Brooke, Carter, and Caden, thanks for giving me the extra time I did not have to write these words and sentences and paragraphs. You lived through them with me. Thanks for the grace to stick around through the good and the bad.

Notes

1. The Way It Has Always Been

1. This saying is frequently misattributed to Voltaire but first appears in Pierre Marc Gaston de Lévis, *Maximes et Réflexions sur Différents sujets de morale et de politique*, 4th ed. (Paris: A. A. Renouard, 1812), 8. In Gaston de Lévis' manuscript, it is also mistakenly attributed to Voltaire.

3. Denial Is Not a Life Strategy

1. Thomas J. Peters, *The Brand You 50: Fifty Ways to Transform Yourself from an "Employee" into a Brand That Shouts* (New York: Alfred A. Knopf, 1999), 42.

2. *Scent of a Woman*, directed by Martin Brest (Universal City, CA: Universal Pictures, 2004), DVD.

4. The Evolution of Ourselves

1. *The Book of Common Prayer* (New York: Seabury Press, 1979), 264.

5. That Which Stays the Same Is Always Changing

1. Charles Darwin never actually said this, but the phrasing appears in an article by Professor Leon Megginson and has run rampant ever since. Leon C. Megginson, "Key to Competition Is Management," *Petroleum Management* 36, no. 1 (1964): 91.

6. The Illusions That Captivate

1. Ayn Rand, *The Fountainhead* (New York: Signet Books, 1971), 23. The quotation is often redacted to read, "The question isn't who is going to let me; it's who is going to stop me."

Conclusion

1. "Prayer for the Diocese," *Book of Common Prayer* (New York: Seabury Press, 1979), 817.

Suggested Reading

James Altucher, *Choose Yourself: Be Happy, Make Millions, Live the Dream (New South Wales, Australia: Lioncrest, 2013)*.

Robert Benson, *The Echo Within* (Colorado Springs: Waterbrook, 2009).

Joseph Campbell, *The Hero with a Thousand Faces (Princeton, NJ: Princeton University Press, 1973)*.

Joseph Campbell with Bill Moyers, *The Power of Myth (New York: Doubleday, 1988)*.

Dr. Henry Cloud, *Necessary Endings: The Employees, Businesses, and Relationships that All of Us Have to Give Up in Oder to Move Forward (New York: HarperCollins, 2010)*.

Seth Godin, *The Dip: A Little Book That Teaches You When to Quit (and When to Stick) (London: Portfolio, 2007)*.

Thich Nhat Hanh, *You Are Here: Discovering the Magic of the Present Moment (Boston: Shambhala, 2009)*.

Robert A Johnson, *Balancing Heaven and Earth: A Memoir of Visions, Dreams, and Realizations (San Francisco: HarperOne, 1998)*.

Alan Jones, *Soul Making: The Desert Way of Spirituality (New York: HarperCollins, 1985)*.

C. G. Jung, *The Archetypes and the Collective Unconscious (Princeton, NJ: Princeton University Press, 1969)*.

Brian D. McLaren, *Everything Must Change: When the World's Biggest Problems and Jesus' Good News Collide* (Nashville: Thomas Nelson, 2009).

Carol Ochs, *Our Lives as Torah: Finding God in Our Stories* (San Francisco: Jossey-Bass, 2001).

Parker J. Palmer, *Let Your Life Speak: Listening for the Voice of Vocation* (San Francisco: Jossey-Bass, 2000).

Tom Peters, *The Brand You 50: Fifty Ways to Transform Yourself from an "Employee" into a Brand That Shouts Distinction, Commitment, and Passion!* (New York: Alfred A. Knopf, 1999).

Rainer Maria Rilke, *Letters to a Young Poet* (New York: W. W. Norton, 1954).

About the Author

Ben Stroup is a writer, consultant, content activist, digital explorer, and senior vice president for fundraising communications at Pursuant, where he helps leaders and organizations develop fully integrated, sustainable publishing models that drive leads, donors, revenue, and engagement.

Ben has written and edited more than thirty books and ebooks, many of them collaborations with key leaders. Some of his latest book projects include *Unconditional Love* (B&H Publishing Group) and *Hope in Front of Me* (with former American Idol finalist Danny Gokey, NavPress).

Ben is a graduate of Belmont University (Nashville, TN). Ben and his wife, Brooke, along with their two boys, Carter and Caden, live in the Nashville, Tennessee, area. You can find Ben online at www.benstroup.com or follow him on Twitter (@ben_stroup), LinkedIn, and Google Plus.